TY

A step-by-step guide to
keyboard mastery

TEACH YOURSELF BOOKS

TYPING

A step-by-step guide to keyboard mastery

Pitmans College

TEACH YOURSELF BOOKS

Hodder and Stoughton

First published 1984
Seventh impression 1989

Copyright © 1984
Pitman Books Ltd

British Library Cataloguing in Publication Data

Pitmans College
    Typing—(Teach yourself books)
    1. Typing
    I. Title
    652.3   Z49

    ISBN 0 340 34308 7

Printed and bound in Great Britain
for Hodder and Stoughton Educational,
a division of Hodder and Stoughton Ltd,
Mill Road, Dunton Green, Sevenoaks, Kent,
by Richard Clay Ltd, Bungay, Suffolk.

Contents

Preface

The skill required by most typists is efficient keyboard operation at reasonable speeds (in which context it must be emphasised that accuracy should not be sacrificed to speed); the ability to decipher manuscript; the preparation of correspondence; and the effective display of tabular and other work. In this book, these and other aspects of the subject are given careful attention.

In recent years, many changes have taken place both in office technology and accepted layouts. Newer styles emphasising simplicity, clarity and speed have gradually replaced more traditional forms. This book brings the subject up-to-date without neglecting the older methods, and will therefore be of interest to typists who want to update their knowledge to keep in step with current trends, as well as to newcomers to typing.

The book has been specially prepared for those who find it inconvenient to attend recognised training centres for personal tuition in the subject. Many who follow its course of instruction will not be particularly concerned with a high speed in typewriting. A good average speed is 40-50 words a minute, and the section on speed tests with its stroke counts will give the learner an opportunity to assess the rate of progress. A good knowledge of touch typewriting can be acquired within a reasonable period, but the skill cannot be gained without considerable personal effort, with daily practice sessions, if possible.

Many facsimile typewritten documents are included and it is confidently believed that those completing the book will have a good working knowledge of typewriting practice whether the machine used be simple or sophisticated.

Introduction

Since the days of the early typewriters there have been remarkable developments and improvements in the manufacture of typewriters, and many different models are now available, including portable typewriters weighing as little as 9 lb (4 kg).

Electrically operated models which produce a particularly clear typescript are widely used today, some of which have a self-correcting device and different symbols for specialised work, as well as a facility to change the pitch (i.e. size of type). Some more sophisticated models, which may be electronically operated, provide a number of facilities similar to those provided by a Word Processor, including an emboldening capability for displaying headings, a memory which allows the typewriter to 'remember' what has previously been typed — ranging from the last few characters or lines to whole paragraphs or pages, depending on the machine — and an opportunity for the typist to use different type faces within one document. Proportional spacing and justifying capabilities are also available, allowing the typist to produce work which gives the appearance of the printed page. These developments have contributed largely to the efficient conduct of administrative work connected with business enterprises and the professions and, at the same time, have relieved the workload of the typist.

There has also been great progress in typewriting instruction, due not only to the provision of better equipment and excellent textbooks prepared specially for students and teachers, but also to the general acceptance of the importance of keyboard knowledge in the rapid expansion of information processing. It is also recognised that many more people should be acquainted with the standard 'Qwerty Keyboard' which is used in computer programming, compositing, electronic typewriting and the visual display unit in offices, airlines, and in many other applications. In this age of modern technology the word *keyboarding* takes on a new meaning.

Whilst recognising, however, that more and more sophisticated machines are coming on to the market, the essential elements of the typewriter remain unchanged. This book concentrates on the operation of manual and electric machines – i.e. those most likely to be used by beginners – whilst at the same time laying a foundation for the learner which remains embedded within modern technology.

1

Touch Typing

The touch method has played an important part in typewriting progress, since it is based on scientific principles. It makes continual movement of the eyes from keyboard to copy and from copy to keyboard unnecessary, as the operator locates the correct keys by touch and not by sight. When the typist becomes proficient, keyboard work is an automatic or subconscious operation.

The word 'touch' cannot be applied in its strictest interpretation. It is not that sense of touch by which a blind reader, for instance, identifies raised braille characters, for each key on the typewriter keyboard feels the same. Rather, the basis of touch typewriting is that each finger operates only those keys allotted to it. Mental confusion and eyestrain are avoided, as the fingers are properly trained to respond accurately to the correct mental impulses set in motion by the sight of the letters to be typed, or even the thought of a word or words to be typed. The fingers move instinctively in correct order as a result of methodical practice, and concentration on the text to be typed.

The standard keyboard

The arrangement of the keyboard is known as the 'Qwerty Keyboard' because of the arrangement of the first six letters of the third row.

The letters of the alphabet are divided into three rows, in the following order:

QWERTYUIOP
ASDFGHJKL
ZXCVBNM

In addition to these alphabet keys there are other keys for figures, fractions, commercial signs and punctuation marks, some of which vary slightly from one model to another. The high degree of standardisation, however, enables the typist to operate any keyboard.

The keyboard is divided into two approximately equal sections, one for each hand. Each section is subdivided into a series of keys for each finger.

Keyboard diagrams

A diagram of the complete keyboard is essential for self-tuition, as it will help in memorising the keys during the early stages of instruction.

On the facing page there is a diagram showing the division of the typewriter keyboard, with an indication of the sections allotted to the fingers of each hand. This diagram should be referred to from time to time during instruction, in order to memorise the location of the keys.

In the chapters dealing with keyboard mastery, diagrams are given at the head of the exercises, showing the particular part of the keyboard on which those exercises are mainly based.

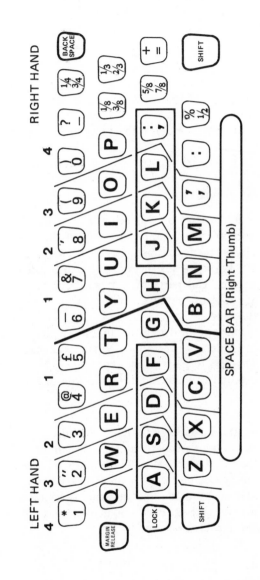

Division of the typewriter keyboard

2

The Parts and Care of the Typewriter

Parts of the typewriter

Before keyboard instruction can begin, it is desirable to become acquainted with the most important parts of the typewriter. The details given below relate to those parts of the machine brought into use during the keyboard instruction, and can be identified in the diagram opposite. The parts of a typewriter may vary slightly between different manufacturers, and the maker's handbook should always be consulted.

The arrangement of the details that follow is alphabetical, and not necessarily in order of operation. When reference is made in subsequent chapters to parts of the typewriter, it will be helpful to refer to this section to understand the function of each part.

Back spacer (1)
This is usually situated at the top of the keyboard, at the extreme right or extreme left with an arrow pointing to the left, or containing the word 'Back-space'. This enables the operator to move the carriage backwards one space at a time. On an electric typewriter, however, the key will repeat its action until pressure is removed. When it is desired to move the carriage back a number of spaces, it is preferable to use the carriage release lever (3).

Bell, warning
The bell rings about six spaces before the point at which the right-hand margin stop has been set.

Carriage (2)

The whole of the mechanism that travels across the top of the machine. On each depression of a key or the space bar, it moves one space from right to left. The carriage frame contains the cylinder (or platen), paper feed rollers, the line space mechanism, and margin and tabulator stops. In many modern machines, however, the type-head (golf ball or daisy wheel) moves while the carriage itself remains stationary.

The parts of the typewriter

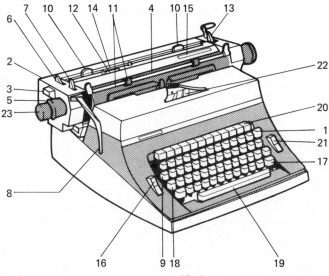

1 Back spacer	12 Paper gauge
2 Carriage	13 Paper release lever
3 Carriage release lever	14 Paper scale
4 Cylinder (or platen)	15 Paper table
5 Cylinder knobs	16 Ribbon switch
6 Interliner	17 Shift keys
7 Line space gauge	18 Shift lock
8 Line space and carriage return lever	19 Space bar
9 Margin release	20 Tabulator key
10 Margin stops	21 Touch control adjuster
11 Paper bail and paper grips	22 Type basket
	23 Variable line spacer

Carriage release lever (3)
This lever may be situated at either or both ends of the carriage and, when depressed, enables the carriage to be moved independently of the escapement either to the right or to the left. It is used mainly when it is necessary to move the carriage a number of spaces beyond the point at which it is already standing – for example, to fill in details on a form or to make a correction.

Cylinder (4)
The cylinder (or platen) is the rubberised roller in the middle of the carriage, and it carries the paper in position.

Cylinder knobs (5)
Twirlers or hand-wheels fitted at each end of the cylinders; they are turned to move the paper into the required position for typing.

Interliner (6)
A lever situated to the left or right of the cylinder which, when moved forwards, frees the cylinder without the line of typing being lost. It is used when typing 'superior' characters or when it is necessary to type on ruled lines.

Line space gauge (7)
This gauge is marked '1', '2', and '3', corresponding to three different line spaces, and the distance that the line space lever rotates the cylinder is determined by the setting of the gauge. There are six single-line spaces to the inch. On most modern typewriters, the line space gauge is marked for half-line spaces as well.

Line space (and carriage return) lever (8)
Used for turning up the paper when desired. At one operation the carriage is returned to the position set and the paper is ready for the beginning of a new line. This lever is struck with the left hand flat (palm downwards), so that the first finger carrying out the operation has the support of the other fingers.

On an electric typewriter the carriage is returned by striking a *key* on the right-hand side. It has a large arrow pointing to the left and is usually a much larger key than the back space. It is operated with the little finger of the right hand.

Margin release (9)
Depression of this key temporarily removes the set margin and permits the extension of the line of writing into the margin. The key may be indicated with an arrow pointing in two directions (left and right) or with the letters MR.

Margin stops (10)
Margins are regulated by the setting of the right-hand and left-hand margin stops at any desired position. These stops prevent movement of the carriage beyond a set point.

'On'/'Off' switch
This is the switch that controls the flow of current to an electric typewriter. It is important to check that the switch is in the 'off' position when the machine is not in use.

Paper bail (11)
The movable bar, which extends the width of the cylinder, on which the typing scale and paper grips are mounted. It holds the paper firmly against the cylinder when the keys are being struck.

Paper grips (11)
Adjustable paper clips or small rollers for holding the paper firmly in position.

Paper gauge (12)
This is an adjustable gauge that ensures that the left-hand edge of the paper is always inserted into the machine at the same point.

Paper release lever (13)
On depression of this lever the paper is free for proper adjustment or for removal from the machine.

Paper scale (14)
A gauge, marked or graduated, to coincide with the letter spaces; it indicates the length of the line of writing. There are twelve letter spaces to the inch in Elite type and ten in Pica type.

Paper table (15)
The paper rests on this metal plate behind the cylinder while it is being

fed through the rollers.

Ribbon switch (16)
There are three positions for this: (i) for using the top half of the ribbon, (ii) for using the lower half of the ribbon, and (iii) for disengaging the ribbon when a stencil is being cut.

Shift keys (17)
One on each side of the keyboard. They change the position of the mechanism so that the capitals or upper-case and miscellaneous characters can be typed.

Shift lock (18)
This temporarily locks the typewriter segment for the continuous writing of capitals or upper-case and miscellaneous characters. By depression of the left shift key the type basket resumes its normal position.

Space bar (19)
The long bar at the bottom of the keyboard. Each time it is depressed the carriage moves one space. It should always be depressed by the righ-hand thumb. On electric typewriters the space bar has a 'repeat' and, while depressed, will cause the carriage to move continuously to any determined point.

Tabulator bar or key (20)
On full depression of this bar or key the carriage moves rapidly to points previously set for the preparation of tabular work. The tabulator bar is set above the top row of keys, while the tabulator key is usually situated on the right-hand side of the keyboard.

Touch control adjuster (21)
A numbered selector switch that may either increase or decrease the tension on the typebars and thus enable the typist to adjust the machine to his or her own touch. If the operator experiences 'jumping' between characters in words, increase of tension will probably be the solution.

Type basket (22)
The name given to the segment that holds all the typebars. It is especially necessary to keep this part of the typewriter clear of eraser dust since otherwise the keys will not function properly.

Variable line spacer (23)
A knob at the end of the cylinder which frees the line space ratchet and allows for any desired spacing between lines of typewritten matter.

Care of the typewriter

A typewriter is an expensive machine, and the efficiency of the service it renders will depend largely on the care taken to keep it in good working order.

Removal
Damage is often due to lack of care when conveying the machine from one table to another. The carriage should be locked in a central position either by the locking device on a portable typewriter or by moving the left- and right-hand margins towards the centre of the carriage. The hands should be placed under each side of the frame, so that they take the full weight, and the typewriter should be carried with the keys away from the body, so that there is no danger of their becoming bent. Never lift the machine by holding each end of the cylinder. Disregard of this instruction may result in serious damage to the machine.

Dust
The chief cause of trouble is dust, and the typewriter should be covered when it is not in use. Any accumulation of dust should be removed daily. When using a rubber eraser, try to prevent the dust from falling into the mechanism: move the carriage as far as possible to the left or to the right, according to the position of the erasure. A long-handled soft brush should be used for removing dust, and dust particles should always be brushed away from the machine.

Oiling
Oil should be applied to the typewriter regularly but sparingly. A

good general rule is to oil points where friction occurs. A wire taper should be dipped into the oil bottle and the lower end applied to the friction point. Wipe away any visible excess. On no account should oil be used on the typebars or in the segment in which the typebars move. Dust will adhere to oil and will cause the typebars to 'stick'. Use the best oil, and obtain it either from a typewriter company or from a firm marketing typewriting accessories.

Cleaning type

The type may become clogged when a new ribbon is in use, and letters that need special attention are the 'closed' letters, such as o, e, a, d, b, g, p, q, etc. An effective way of removing the dirt is by the application of a little benzine on the typefaces. A type brush should be used, and the movement should be forwards and backwards, not across the type basket which contains the typebars. There are also various mechanical cleaners on the market which can be bought from any office stationers. It is recommended that type should be cleaned before and after cutting a stencil.

Repairs

The question of repairs is seldom dealt with in typewriting manuals. It is possible for an experienced typist to make minor adjustments, but when a machine is manipulated with care there is usually little need for the services of the typewriter mechanic. If, however, any serious defect develops, do not interfere with the mechanism but obtain the services of a skilled mechanic.

3

Preliminaries to Keyboard Mastery

The main parts of the machine have now been noted, but there are still some important matters to be considered before keyboard operation can begin.

Position at machine

To carry out any machine work in an efficient manner it is generally agreed that a comfortable position will ensure complete command during operation, and the typewriter is no exception.

Furniture most suited for typewriting cannot always be secured, but an attempt should be made to adjust the height of the table and chair so that it is possible to sit comfortably. Wooden blocks, foot-rests and cushions can be used for this purpose. The beginner should sit with the elbows near the sides of the body and the forearms parallel to the slope of the typewriter keyboard.

When the machine has been placed with the bottom edge of the frame approximately in line with the front of the table, the typist should adopt a natural and easy position before the machine, with the body inclined slightly forwards. It is advisable to have an adjustable chair, fitted with a back-rest but without arms, otherwise the proper movement of the forearms will be impeded.

During the depression of the keys, the backs of the hands should be kept perfectly level with the slope of the keyboard and the fingers should be bent at the middle joint. There should be very little movement of the wrist.

The feet should rest firmly on the floor, one slightly in front of the other in order to give balance to the body.

It is important that the typewriting table should be in a good light. The copy should be placed on the right-hand side of the machine so that the vision is not obstructed when the carriage return lever is operated, and care should be taken to ensure that shadows do not fall on the copy.

Paper insertion and removal

The method of inserting the paper is a simple operation and can be performed rapidly. Hold the paper to be inserted with the left hand and place it behind the cylinder so that it rests lightly on the feed rolls – the small rollers between the paper table and the cylinder. Ensure that the left-hand edge of the paper is against the paper gauge at '0'. Then 'swish' the paper into position with a quick turn of the right-hand cylinder knob. If the paper has not fed in evenly, it can be adjusted by using the paper release lever.

Withdrawal of the paper should also be done rapidly. The paper should be held at the top left-hand corner between the thumb and first finger of the left hand and lightly pulled at the same time as the paper release lever is operated. The paper can thus be removed quietly from the machine.

The backing sheet

An improvement in the appearance of the typewritten work will be secured by the use of a backing sheet – a sheet of stout paper placed behind the typewriting paper – particularly when only one sheet of paper is required in the machine. A backing sheet helps to preserve the even surface of the cylinder, and a mark on the backing sheet will indicate when the bottom of the paper is being approached. A backing sheet ruled to show the side margins can also be helpful.

Depression of keys

Cultivate a light touch. Do not push or press the keys; tap them with a light, quick blow, and this will ensure a clear and sharp impression. After a little practice the operator will be able to judge the degree of pressure that is necessary to obtain the best result. The finger must leave the key immediately on depression, so that the typebar is not restricted in its downward movement. Punctuation marks require a lighter touch than that used for the other keys. A heavy depression of the full stop, comma and hyphen is likely to puncture the paper.

The operator of an electric typewriter requires considerably less force than a manual machine and the hands tend to be held flatter because the keyboard is less steep. Pressure is regulated by the machine.

Rhythm

The beginner will find it helpful when learning new key reaches to type each letter to a conscious rhythm. Tap at one stroke a second on the table for, say, thirty seconds for an appreciation of what constitutes a speed of one stroke a second, and then increase the rate to two strokes a second. These are the speeds recommended for exercises in the keyboard mastery sections. However, as the typing skill develops, it will be found that rhythm has less to do with the metronomic typing of each letter and more to do with the patterns contained within words and word groups.

Type sizes

The sizes of typewriter type in most general use are Elite and Pica. There are twelve letters to the inch for Elite type. Pica type is a larger type, and there are ten letters to the inch. The exercises in the keyboard mastery sections are shown in Pica type. It will require a very elementary arithmetical calculation to ascertain the space required for a line containing a similar number of letters of Pica and Elite. A line of writing containing sixty characters (or a space in lieu of a character) of Pica type will occupy six inches, but the same number of characters in Elite type will take up only five inches.

Paper

International Paper Sizes A4 ($8\frac{1}{4}$ in $\times$ $11\frac{3}{4}$ in; 210 mm $\times$ 297 mm) and A5 ($5\frac{7}{8}$ in $\times$ $8\frac{1}{4}$ in; 148 mm $\times$ 210 mm) are in common use in Britain.

Good-quality paper is always more economical since both sides can be used.

The following table gives the number of spaces across a page of A4 and A5 in both Elite and Pica, and the number of lines to the page.

	A4	*A5* (shorter side at top)	*A5* (longer side at top)
Spaces across the page			
Elite (12 to 2.5 cm or 1 in)	100	70	100
Pica (10 to 2.5 cm or 1 in)	82	59	82
Lines down the page			
Elite and Pica (both 6 lines to the inch)	70	50	35

Different styles in typewritten material

That typewriting should be done by 'touch' is beyond dispute, but apart from definite methods of operation, there are few hard-and-fast rules regarding the production of an ordinary piece of typescript. However, the blocked method of layout, whereby all the lines of letters and other documents begin at the left-hand margin, is in wide use. This method saves time and has a clear, pleasing appearance. Open punctuation, which is usually used in conjunction with blocked layout, saves further time and will also be discussed later in the book (page 75).

The more traditional styles, involving indented paragraphs (usually $\frac{1}{2}$ inch – 5–6 spaces – from the left-hand margin), centred headings, etc., are still preferred by some, and individual organisations will often specify the style to be used.

Whatever the method, consistency is important.

4

Keyboard Mastery: The Second Row

The most important section of the typewriter keyboard will naturally receive first consideration. It consists of eight keys in the second row from the space bar, known as the 'home keys', and from these keys the sense of location of all the other keys will be developed.

These home keys are **a s d f** for the fingers of the left hand and **; l k j** for the fingers of the right hand. They are often referred to as the 'guide keys', although it is generally considered that the guide keys are the two home keys operated by the little fingers – **a** and **;**. The following diagram shows the arrangement of the home keys (the boxed-in sections):

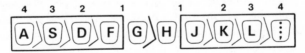

During keyboard operation the tips of the fingers indicated in the diagram should rest lightly (so lightly that there is no actual depression of the keys) on the home keys. The little finger of the left hand operates **a**, and the third, second and first fingers the remaining keys for the left section – **s d f**. The little finger of the right hand operates the semicolon (**;**), and the third, second and first fingers the remaining keys for the right section – **l k j**.

Repeat aloud several times **a s d f** and **; l k j**, in this order, and during the repetition tap the respective fingers on the table at equal intervals of time – one tap a second – as mentioned under 'Rhythm' on page 13. This will give a clear picture of what is required.

Then feed a sheet of paper (with backing sheet) into the machine for the first exercise; set the margin stops at 25 and 75 (Elite type) or

16 and 76 (Pica type), and return the carriage to the left-hand margin stop for the beginning of the first line. Set the line space gauge for single-line spacing.

Place your fingers on the home keys, as shown on the diagram on page 15. Every time you remove your left hand from the keyboard to return the carriage at the end of a line, or operate the carriage-return key on an electric typewriter, you must be able to return your fingers to their home keys *without looking at the keyboard*.

Each key should be struck lightly and at equal intervals of time – one stroke a second until repeated practice makes an increase to two strokes a second possible. It is essential at this stage that there should be absolute accuracy and even depression of the keys; speed will come with regular practice.

Place the copy on the right-hand side of the typewriter. This will prevent the copy from being hidden by the left forearm when the carriage is returned. Make sure that it is in such a position that you can read the exercises easily without having to alter your position at the machine.

The four keys memorised for the left hand (**a s d f**) are required for the first line of Exercise 1, and, with the eyes on the copy, this combination of letters is to be repeated twelve times. While the home keys for the left hand are being struck for this first line, the fingers of the right hand should be resting lightly on their respective home keys. The line numbers are inserted for reference only, and the reminders given with the exercises should be carefully noted before starting to type.

When the end of each line is reached, the carriage on manual machines should be returned to the right of the machine by contacting the carriage return lever with the side of the first finger of the left hand (palm downwards); this finger should be supported by the other fingers of this hand. If this lever is struck smartly, the double action of turning up the paper for the next line and returning the carriage to the left-hand margin stop will be accomplished.

During the return of the carriage, the right hand keeps its home key position and the left hand returns to the home keys immediately on completion of the carriage return movement.

Now note the second line. This deals with the four keys memorised for the right hand (**; l k j**) and completes the eight home keys. The fingers of the left hand should be in the normal home keys position during the typing of the second line.

In the third and fourth lines the additional keys (**g** and **h**) are introduced; they are shown in the diagram at the head of the exercises. The first finger of the left hand will move slightly to the right from **f** to **g**, and the first finger of the right hand will move slightly to the left from **j** to **h**. The other fingers should not be moved when the additional key is struck. Immediately after the depression of **g** or **h** the finger should return to its home key. Each series of letters in these lines finishes on the home keys for the first fingers – **f** and **j**.

For the fifth and sixth lines the order has been varied. Repeated practice will ensure that, as each letter is read, the appropriate finger will respond to the direction by the brain and depress the key for the letter shown in the copy.

A space is required after each series of letters in the fifth and sixth lines, and the space bar should always be struck with the right-hand thumb, but the fingers should not leave their home key positions. The time taken for the depression of the space bar should be equal to that for a letter or character key; in this way correct rhythm will be maintained.

Each line in the exercises should be treated as a separate item and copied three times. For repetition practice, type in single-line spacing. After the repeated practice on each line, type in double-line spacing at least one accurate copy of the whole exercise.

More work with the space bar is given in Exercise 2, and Exercises 3 and 4 consist of words built up from the home keys and the additional keys for the first finger of each hand.

After finishing each exercise examine the work and circle any mistakes in pencil. Find out the cause of any errors – uneven key depression, wrong fingering, etc. – and then type the corrections several times. If any of the typed letters are 'shadowed', it can be assumed that the keys are being pressed, instead of being tapped with a staccato movement.

Apart from the question of accuracy, work produced on a manual machine should be examined from the point of view of evenness of touch. There should not be varying shades of thickness; each letter should have the appearance of having had the same intensity of depression. If some fingers appear to be weak (and very often this is the case with the little fingers), there should be additional practice with the letters that show any such weakness.

Exercise 1

1. asdfasdfasdfasdfasdfasdfasdfasdf
2. ;lkj;lkj;lkj;lkj;lkj;lkj;lkj;lkj
3. asdfgfasdfgfasdfgfasdfgfasdfgf
4. ;lkjhj;lkjhj;lkjhj;lkjhj;lkjhj
5. fdsa jkl; fdsa jkl; fdsa dfas kj;l dfas
6. sfad lj;k sfad lj;k sfad sadf l;kj sadf l;kj sadf

Exercise 2

1. as ad af ag ;l ;k ;j ;h as ad af ag ;l ;k ;j ;h
2. ;l ;k ;j ;h as ad af ag ;l ;k ;j ;h as ad af ag
3. as ;l ad ;k af ;j ag ;h as ;l ad ;k af ;j ag ;h
4. sa l; da k; fa j; ga h; sa l; da k; fa j; ga h;
5. sd df sd df lk kj lk kj sd df sd df lk kj lk kj
6. gf fg gf fg jh hj jh hj gf fg gf fg jh hj jh hj

Reminders: set margin stops at 25 and 75 (Elite type) or 16 and 66 (Pica type); adopt correct position at keyboard; do not look at keyboard; fingers to rest lightly on home keys; right-hand thumb for space bar depression; equal intervals between each key depression; one stroke a second; the line numbers are for reference only. Type each line three times.

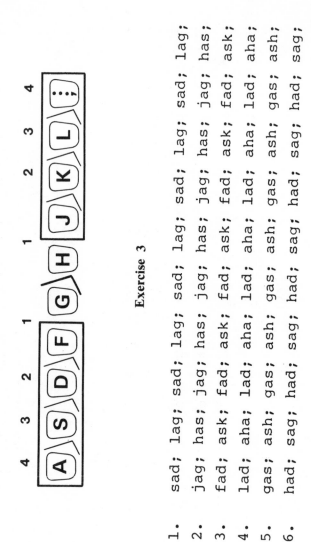

Exercise 3

1. sad; lag; sad; lag; sad; lag; sad; lag;
2. jag; has; jag; has; jag; has; jag; has;
3. fad; ask; fad; ask; fad; ask; fad; ask;
4. lad; aha; lad; aha; lad; aha; lad; aha;
5. gas; ash; gas; ash; gas; ash; gas; ash;
6. had; sag; had; sag; had; sag; had; sag;

Exercise 4

1. dash; half; dash; half; dash; half; dash; half;
2. lass; glad; lass; glad; lass; glad; lass; glad;
3. gall; shag; gall; shag; gall; shag; gall; shag;
4. flask shall flask shall flask shall flask shall
5. salad glass salad glass salad glass salad glass
6. galas flags galas flags galas flags galas flags

Reminders: set margin stops at 25 and 75 (Elite type) or 16 and 66 (Pica type); right-hand thumb for space bar depression; first finger returns to home key after striking additional key; little movement of the wrists. Type each line three times.

Finally, remember that this first stage of keyboard mastery is of special importance; it is with this second row of keys that the remainder of the keyboard is associated, and extended practice on the exercises will be well worth the time spent in this way.

5

Keyboard Mastery: The Third Row

The third row of the keyboard includes ten additional letters of the alphabet, five for the fingers of each hand. The order in which they appear is shown in the following diagram:

When the correct position at the machine has been taken up and the fingers have been placed on the home keys, the keys of the third row can be operated and memorised. They are in a position above and slightly to the left of their corresponding keys in the second row. An examination of the keyboard diagram on page 3 or the diagram at the head of the exercises in this section will show the direction of the movement required.

In order to associate correctly the keys of the second and third rows, the first practice will be to reach from the home keys to the third row. With the little finger of the left hand strike the guide key **a**. With the same finger reach upwards and slightly to the left to strike the **q** key, and then return the finger to the second row and again strike the key for **a**. The movements should be repeated several times, with a space between each series of letters, as:

aqa aqa aqa aqa aqa aqa aqa aqa

A similar movement will then be made by the third, second and first fingers for this association of keys for the left hand, as:

```
sws  sws  sws  sws  sws  sws  sws  sws
ded  ded  ded  ded  ded  ded  ded  ded
frf  frf  frf  frf  frf  frf  frf  frf
```

When the key in the third row is being struck, only the operating finger should move upwards, the remainder keeping their home key positions. This movement is a little difficult at first, but, with the hands extended and the finger tips resting lightly on the table, the finger movements can be practised away from the keyboard.

In the second row the first finger of the left hand was allotted an additional key (**g**), and there is a corresponding key (**t**) in the third row for the same finger. Strike the home key **f**; with an upward and slightly right movement strike the key for **t**, and then return the finger to the second row and strike the key for **f**. Practise this exercise several times, as:

```
ftf  ftf  ftf  ftf  ftf  ftf  ftf  ftf
```

The four fingers of the right hand should have been on their respective home keys (**; l k j**) and ready for action. With the little finger strike the key for the semicolon; then, with an upward and slightly left movement, strike the key for **p** and return the finger to strike the guide key, as:

```
;p;  ;p;  ;p;  ;p;  ;p;  ;p;  ;p;  ;p;
```

The same movements should then be followed with regard to the other home keys for this hand and the associated keys in the third row, as:

```
lol  lol  lol  lol  lol  lol  lol  lol
kik  kik  kik  kik  kik  kik  kik  kik
juj  juj  juj  juj  juj  juj  juj  juj
```

The first finger of the right hand was called upon to operate an additional key (**h**) in the second row, and there is a corresponding key (**y**) in the third row for the same finger. Strike the home key **j**; with an upward and slightly left movement strike **y**, and then return the finger to the second row and strike the key for **j**. The following exercise should be typed several times, with an intervening space, as:

jyj jyj jyj jyj jyj jyj jyj jyj

So far, this preliminary practice has required the use of each hand separately. The disengaged hand should have remained in the home key position, except, of course, for the return of the carriage.

Exercise 5 is based on the above directions, and the last two lines contain the additional keys for the first fingers. Instead of repeated practice on one series of letters, alternate use is made of each hand. This will give a balanced effect to the keyboard work.

In Exercise 6 the series of letters in the first five lines begin in the second row and finish in the third row. The finger should return to the second row as each series is completed. In the sixth line each series begins and ends on the third row of keys.

Exercise 7 consists of words formed from letters in the second and third rows, and in the first two lines the words require alternate use of each hand. In the third, fourth and fifth lines alternate use is made of letters in the right and left sections of the keyboard. This exercise ends with a selection of words with double letters. The double letters should be typed with the same regularity as keys for different letters.

Short sentences in Exercise 8 complete the section, but the capital letter and full stop ordinarily required will be introduced at a later stage.

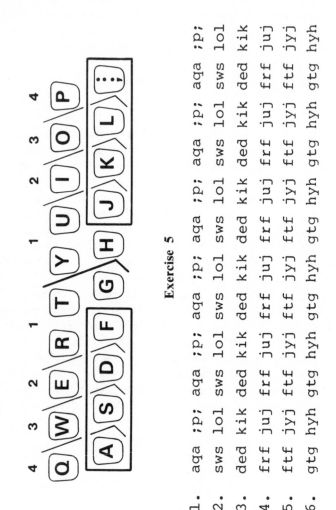

Exercise 5

1. aqa ;p; aqa ;p; aqa ;p; aqa ;p; aqa ;p;
2. sws lol sws lol sws lol sws lol sws lol
3. ded kik ded kik ded kik ded kik ded kik
4. frf juj frf juj frf juj frf juj frf juj
5. ftf jyj ftf jyj ftf jyj ftf jyj ftf jyj
6. gtg hyh gtg hyh gtg hyh gtg hyh gtg hyh

Exercise 6

1. aqw ;po aqw ;po aqw ;po aqw ;po aqw ;po
2. swe loi swe loi swe loi swe loi swe loi
3. der kiu der kiu der kiu der kiu der kiu
4. frt juy frt juy frt juy frt juy frt juy
5. gtr hyu gtr hyu gtr hyu gtr hyu gtr hyu
6. qaw p;o wse oli edr iku qaw p;o wse oli edr iku

*Reminders: set margin stops at 25 and 75 (Elite type) or 16 and 66 (Pica type);
find home keys position without looking at the keyboard; the touch should be as
light as possible; time for depression of space bar the same as for character key;
examine work, encircle all errors and type corrections several times. Type each
line three times.*

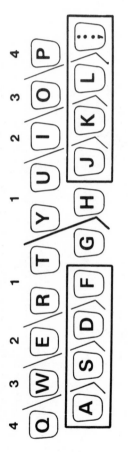

Exercise 7

1. dear poll feat jill gear oily tear holy read hill
2. hoop star hull deaf loop dare pulp gate pill fret
3. lap fit hay pay dog key for hey fur jay foe; fig;
4. flay dial work goal fury girl dual dish fowl quay
5. spelt prowl shape lapel shale palsy queue; furls;
6. ladder dapper fitter sallow ferret dagger gossip;

Exercise 8

1. they are sure that they were right at that period
2. at their request the first few words were deleted
3. there is a good supply of hot water at this hotel
4. goods like those are sure to get you the top rate
5. he helped us to pass the press proofs of the list
6. the guard said that the lads had paid their fares

Reminders: set margin stops at 25 and 75 (Elite type) or 16 and 66 (Pica type); the hand not typing should remain in home keys position; examine work for accuracy and evenness of touch. Type each line three times.

6

Keyboard Mastery: The First Row

With the ability at this stage to type words and sentences there will be a natural feeling of progress. If the exercises have been typed accurately and rhythmically, that feeling will be well justified, and the remaining letters of the alphabet can now be learnt. These letters are in the first row of the keyboard (just above the space bar), and they appear in the following order:

The first row will be memorised by its association with the home keys, and the movement necessary, which is downwards and slightly to the left, should be practised several times. The little finger of the left hand has no letter or character key in this row, but it is given the work of operating the shift key. This key is used for typing capitals and miscellaneous characters, and will be fully explained in a later chapter.

After finding the home keys without looking at the keyboard, strike the guide key **a**; then with the little finger, depress fully the shift key and release it. The time taken for the depression of the shift key should be the same as for a character key. Accurate timing of the stroke for the shift key will be secured with repeated practice. After this shift key operation the little finger returns to strike the guide key

a. The shift key depression does not move the carriage one space, and the typewritten work for this action will be a repetition of the guide key **a**. Count *one—two—three* while carrying out the movement.

Now with the third finger strike **s**; lower to strike **z** and then return to strike **s**. Repeat these movements accurately several times, with a space between each series, and the line will appear as:

```
szs  szs  szs  szs  szs  szs  szs  szs
szs  szs  szs  szs  szs  szs  szs  szs
```

Similar movements by the second and first fingers from the other home keys for this hand will give:

```
dxd  dxd  dxd  dxd  dxd  dxd  dxd  dxd
fcf  fcf  fcf  fcf  fcf  fcf  fcf  fcf
dxd  dxd  dxd  dxd  dxd  dxd  dxd  dxd
fcf  fcf  fcf  fcf  fcf  fcf  fcf  fcf
```

There is an additional key for the first finger; it is that for **v**, and its home key in the second row is **f**:

```
fvf  fvf  fvf  fvf  fvf  fvf  fvf  fvf
fvf  fvf  fvf  fvf  fvf  fvf  fvf  fvf
```

This completes the work for the left hand, and the practice will be continued for the right hand.

First, strike the semicolon, the guide key in the second row; then downwards and to the left for the full stop, and back to the semicolon, as:

```
;.; ;.; ;.; ;.; ;.; ;.; ;.; ;.;
;.; ;.; ;.; ;.; ;.; ;.; ;.; ;.;
```

Continue this practice for the remaining home keys, as:

```
l,l l,l l,l l,l l,l l,l l,l l,l
kmk kmk kmk kmk kmk kmk kmk kmk
jnj jnj jnj jnj jnj jnj jnj jnj
l,l l,l l,l l,l l,l l,l l,l l,l
kmk kmk kmk kmk kmk kmk kmk kmk
jnj jnj jnj jnj jnj jnj jnj jnj
```

The additional key in the first row for the first finger of the right hand is **b**, and·its home key in the second row is **j**:

```
jbj jbj jbj jbj jbj jbj jbj jbj
jbj jbj jbj jbj jbj jbj jbj jbj
```

In the first five lines of Exercise 9 the series of letters already practised are given in alternate form. An asterisk in the first line indicates the depression of the shift key with the little finger of the left hand, but there will be no space movement for this depression. The sixth line deals only with characters in the first row.

For Exercise 10 the movements are varied, and each series in the first five lines ends with a key in the first row. The fingers will automatically return to the home key positions from the other rows, since each series begins with a key in the second row, but in the sixth line the reach is from the first row to the third row.

In the first two lines of Exercise 11 the words contain only letters from the first and second rows. In the remaining lines letters from all three rows of the keyboard are included, and each word requires alternate use of the right and left sections of the keyboard.

The first five words in each line of Exercise 12 are typed on alternate sides of the keyboard and repeated. They provide another example of the disengaged hand remaining in the home keys position while the other hand is striking the keys.

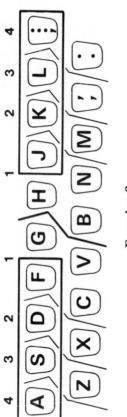

Exercise 9

1. a*a ;•; a*a ;•; a*a ;•; a*a ;•;
2. szs l,l szs l,l szs l,l szs l,l
3. dxd kmk dxd kmk dxd kmk dxd kmk
4. fcf jnj fcf jnj fcf jnj fcf jnj
5. fvf jbj fvf jbj fvf jbj fvf jbj
6. zxz ,m, cvc nbn. zxz ,m, cvc nbn

Exercise 10

1. asz ;l, asz ;l, asz ;l, asz ;l, asz ;l, asz ;l,
2. sdx lkm sdx lkm sdx lkm sdx lkm sdx lkm sdx lkm
3. dfc kjn dfc kjn dfc kjn dfc kjn dfc kjn dfc kjn
4. fgv jhb fgv jhb fgv jhb fgv jhb fgv jhb fgv jhb
5. aqz ;p. swz lo, dex kim frc jun gtv hyb aqz ;p.
6. zqz .p. zwz ,o, xex mim crc nun vtv byb zqz .p.

Reminders: set margin stops at 25 and 75 (Elite type) or 16 and 66 (Pica type); eyes on copy; note downward movement from second row; full depression of shift key in the same time as that taken for character key; Exercise 9, line 1 indicates the depression of the shift key. Type each line three times.

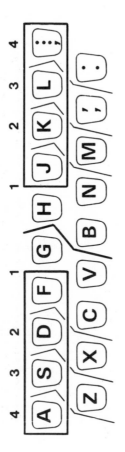

Exercise 11

1. cab ham van dab nag jam sac ban sax cad jab fan
2. and can mad lax bag jag bad nab cam lac dam man
3. amend label flame japan panel glebe brick snake
4. visor broth clays urban vodka angle lapel endow
5. chair mango docks neigh gland shame anent slant
6. spend penal chant handy smelt chaos bench cycle

Exercise 12

1. face limb raze boil axes face limb raze boil axes
2. card bulk aver lion fact card bulk aver lion fact
3. dace join cave kink arcs dace join cave kink arcs
4. gave plum tact bulb vast gave plum tact bulb vast
5. daze milk wave puny sect daze milk wave puny sect
6. save hymn cart inky aces save hymn cart inky aces

*Reminders: set margin stops at 25 and 75 (Elite type) or 16 and 66 (Pica type);
cultivate a light and even touch; do not look at the keyboard—eyes on the copy;
examine typewritten work, encircle errors and type correct words. Type each
line three times.*

7

Keyboard Mastery: The Top Row

Up to this point the keyboard work has been connected with the twenty-six letters of the alphabet (not the capitals), and with the punctuation marks for the semicolon, comma and full stop.

This section will include the fourth (or top) row of keys, which introduces the arabic numerals (**1** to **0**) and the hyphen. On some machines keys are not provided for **1** and **0**, and the figures may be obtained by typing the small letter '**l**' for **1** and the capital letter '**O**' for zero. A capital letter '**I**' should not be used to represent the arabic number '**1**'. It will be seen in the following diagram of this row of keys that other signs are given, but at the moment work is concerned only with the bottom portions of the keys.

The first fingers of each hand will continue their dual task, and the four middle keys have to be operated by these two fingers.

Hitherto, the reach from the home keys has been the width between one row, but for this top row a longer span is necessary. A glance at the diagram at the head of the exercises will show that, after leaving the third row, the movement from that row to the top is slightly to the left of the corresponding key in the third row. The movement necessary will be fully impressed on the mind by practice which combines the second row with the third and top rows.

Begin with the fingers resting lightly on the home keys. Strike the guide key **a**, then strike **q**, return the finger to **a**, and then move the finger upwards and slightly to the left to strike **l**.

aq1 aq1 aq1 aq1 aq1 aq1 aq1 aq1

Similar practice for the remaining home keys of the left hand and the corresponding keys of the third and top rows will give the following:

sw2 sw2 sw2 sw2 sw2 sw2 sw2 sw2
de3 de3 de3 de3 de3 de3 de3 de3
fr4 fr4 fr4 fr4 fr4 fr4 fr4 fr4

For the first finger the additional key is **5**, and this should be typed with its associated keys in the other rows, as:

gt5 gt5 gt5 gt5 gt5 gt5 gt5 gt5

This completes the operation for the left hand, and the movements will be similar for the fingers of the right hand, which should have been in the home keys position during the typing of the previous lines.

Now for the right-hand practice, with the left hand in the home keys position. Strike the semicolon, the guide key for the right hand; reach upwards and strike **p**, return the finger to its home key, and then reach upwards and slightly to the left to strike **o**.

;p0 ;p0 ;p0 ;p0 ;p0 ;p0 ;p0 ;p0

4 3 2 1   1 2 3 4

| * / 1 | " / 2 | ´ / 3 | @ / 4 | £ / 5 | ‾ / 6 | & / 7 | ´ / 8 | (/ 9 |) / 0 | ? / - |

Q W E R T Y U I O P

Exercise 13

1. aq1 ;p0 aq1 ;p0 aq1 ;p0 aq1 ;p0 aq1 ;p0
2. sw2 lo9 sw2 lo9 sw2 lo9 sw2 lo9 sw2 lo9
3. de3 ki8 de3 ki8 de3 ki8 de3 ki8 de3 ki8
4. fr4 ju7 fr4 ju7 fr4 ju7 fr4 ju7 fr4 ju7
5. gt5 hy6 gt5 hy6 gt5 hy6 gt5 hy6 gt5 hy6
6. aq1 ;p0 sw2 lo9 de3 ki8 fr4 ju7 gt5 hy6 aq1 ;p0

Exercise 14

1. a1a ;0; a1a ;0; a1a ;0; a1a ;0; a1a ;0;
2. s2s 191 s2s 191 s2s 191 s2s 191 s2s 191
3. d3d k8k d3d k8k d3d k8k d3d k8k d3d k8k
4. f4f j7j f4f j7j f4f j7j f4f j7j f4f j7j
5. g5g h6h g5g h6h g5g h6h g5g h6h g5g h6h
6. 13 24 25 26 27 28 29 30 3- 34 45 56 67 78 89 90

*Reminders: set margin stops at 25 and 75 (Elite type) or 16 and 66 (Pica type);
note movement from second row to the top row; the letter 'l' may be used for the
numeral 'one'; lighter depression of punctuation marks.*

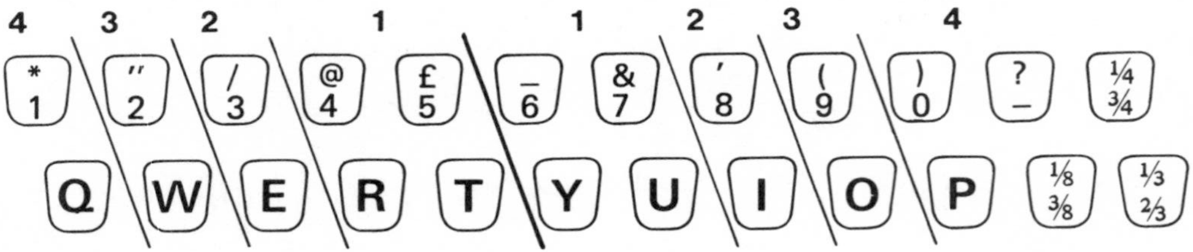

Keyboard diagram (top row keys shown):

```
4 [* 1]  3 [" 2]  2 [/ 3]  1 [@ 4]  [£ 5]  [- 6]  1 [& 7]  2 [' 8]  3 [( 9]  4 [) 0]  [? -]
                                                                              [⅛ ⅜]  [¼ ¾]
                                                                                     [⅓ ⅔]
[Q] [W] [E] [R] [T] [Y] [U] [I] [O] [P]
```

Exercise 15

1. tip 123 pit 345 try 678 wit 890 pry 345 yet 678
2. out 132 top 354 pit 687 ere 809 pro 354 tie 687
3. rye 213 pot 435 toe 768 pep 980 roe 435 pow 768
4. ewe 231 pop 453 eye 786 woe 809 yew 453 two 786
5. you 312 put 534 wet 867 pie 800 wry 534 pup 867
6. rut 321 tow 543 rue 876 ire 900 toy 543 pip 876

Exercise 16

1.	tree	1234	weep	3456	peer	5678	quip	7890	prop	1234
2.	peep	1324	weir	3546	tory	5768	wiry	7980	tyre	1324
3.	type	1342	quit	3564	writ	5786	tyro	8790	wire	1342
4.	your	2134	true	4356	wipe	6578	poor	8709	rite	2134
5.	port	2143	trip	4365	tire	6587	pity	8907	troy	2143
6.	rope	2341	wept	4563	pert	6785	tort	9780	tour	2341

Reminders: set margin stops at 25 and 75 (Elite type) or 16 and 66 (Pica type);
all words contain letters in third row only; numerals in top row; keep eyes on
copy during keyboard operation; encircle all errors and type corrections several
times.

Follow this form of practice for the remaining home keys and their associated keys in the third and top rows, as:

```
lo9 lo9 lo9 lo9 lo9 lo9 lo9 lo9
ki8 ki8 ki8 ki8 ki8 ki8 ki8 ki8
ju7 ju7 ju7 ju7 ju7 ju7 ju7 ju7
```

The additional key for the first finger is **6**, and this is associated with **h** and **y** in the other rows, as:

```
hy6 hy6 hy6 hy6 hy6 hy6 hy6 hy6
```

The instruction up to this stage has dealt with forty of the forty-six keys, and the six remaining keys (mainly fractions) are operated by the little finger of the right hand.

The movements from and to the home keys row are similar to those already observed for the keys of the first three rows.

In Exercise 13 the above movements have been embodied, but each series is arranged to give alternate work on the left and right sections of the keyboard. For Exercise 14 the work is arranged so that the fingers reach from the second row to the top row and back to the second row. The sixth line deals only with the top row.

Further practice for this chapter is provided in Exercise 15, which consists of three-letter words built up exclusively of letters contained in the third row, and also a series of three numerals from the top row. The same procedure is followed in Exercise 16, the difference being four-letter words and a series of four numerals.

8

Shift Keys and Shift Lock – Combination Characters and Special Signs

Shift keys and shift lock

Each of the forty-six character keys operate typebars on which are fitted two characters, and they may include a small (lower-case) and capital (upper-case) alphabetical character, a figure, a commercial sign, a punctuation mark or a fraction. The keyboard diagram on page 3 shows all the miscellaneous characters and signs on the top portion of the keys.

For these capital letters and miscellaneous characters the shift keys are necessary – they move the cylinder or the type segments for the correct type impression. There is a shift key on each side of the keyboard, usually at each end of the bottom row of keys. The shift keys are operated by the little fingers. If the character required is on the right-hand side of the keyboard, the left shift key must be depressed, and vice versa.

Careful practice is essential to secure correct depression of the shift key. It is different from that for the ordinary key depression, as the shift key is fully depressed and held down during the striking of the character key on the opposite side of the keyboard. The timing of this depression should be the same as for a character key – and ensure that there is no break in the rhythm. The finger should return to its normal home key position immediately the shift key is released.

The shift lock is depressed when several capital letters are to be typed in succession.

The first practice for shift key operation will deal with associated keys of the second, third and fourth rows. The capitals (use of shift keys) are given for the second row, the lower-case letters for the third row and the miscellaneous characters (use of shift keys) for the fourth row. On some machines, the keys may differ from those shown for the top row. The appropriate alterations should therefore be made.

Depress the right-hand shift key to its full extent and use the little finger of the left hand to type **A**; release the shift key and then type the lower-case letter in the third row for the same finger **q**, and again depress the right-hand shift key to type the asterisk (*) in the top row. Repeat these movements several times, as:

Aq* Aq* Aq* Aq* Aq* Aq* Aq* Aq*

Now combine the remaining keys for the left hand in the three rows under consideration, as:

```
Sw"  Sw"  Sw"  Sw"  Sw"  Sw"  Sw"  Sw"
De/  De/  De/  De/  De/  De/  De/  De/
Fr@  Fr@  Fr@  Fr@  Fr@  Fr@  Fr@
Gt£  Gt£  Gt£  Gt£  Gt£  Gt£  Gt£  Gt£
```

Similar movements by the right hand and the depression of the left-hand shift key will complete the remaining six upper-case characters of the top row. Type six lines, as:

```
:p)  :p)  :p)  :p)  :p)  :p)  :p)  :p)
:p?  :p?  :p?  :p?  :p?  :p?  :p?  :p?
Lo(  Lo(  Lo(  Lo(  Lo(  Lo(  Lo(  Lo(
Ki'  Ki'  Ki'  Ki'  Ki'  Ki'  Ki'  Ki'
Ju&  Ju&  Ju&  Ju&  Ju&  Ju&  Ju&  Ju&
Hy_  Hy_  Hy_  Hy_  Hy_  Hy_  Hy_  Hy_
```

Upper-case characters are contained in the three outside character keys of the bottom (or first) row; they are on the typebars already operated for the comma, full stop and $\frac{1}{2}$ fraction. The comma usually appears twice on one typebar, as does the full stop. Over the $\frac{1}{2}$ fraction is usually the per cent sign.

Depress the left-hand shift key to its full extent, and with the third finger strike the key for the bottom row (the comma); with the little finger strike the key to the right (the full stop), without shift key depression, and again depress the shift key while the little finger moves to the right to strike the key for the per cent sign, as:

,.% ,.% ,.% ,.% ,.% ,.% ,.% ,.%

Ordinarily, it would not be necessary to release the shift key for the full stop, but the above combination is given for practice in the use of the shift key.

In Exercise 17 the first line deals with the practice work of this section, and the second line involves the operation of the same keys but using the shift key in a different order. For the initial capitals in the third line the left-hand shift key will be required and for the fourth line the right-hand shift key. In the fifth and sixth lines three-letter words are given alternately for the left and right sections of the keyboard.

Exercise 18 consists of words arranged for alternate use of the right and left shift keys.

All the alphabet letters, punctuation marks and miscellaneous characters are included in Exercise 19, which provides excellent practice covering the major part of the keyboard. The shift lock will be used when underscoring in the third line.

Exercise 20 is arranged for shift lock practice, and the lock will have to be released for the typing of the dash (or hyphen) between the items in the list of subjects.

The top row containing arabic numerals and miscellaneous characters is not easy to memorise, and the diagram given at the head of the exercises in this chapter includes this row and shows its association with the third row.

Roman numerals

When roman numerals are required, they are compiled from the following letters – capital or small:

```
I   (1);      V      (5);      X   (10);
L  (50);      C   (100);       D  (500);
              M  (1000);
```

Exercise 17

1. Aq* :p) Sw" Lo(De/ Ki' Fr@ Ju& Gt£ Hy_ :p? ,.%
2. aQ1 ;P0 sW2 1O9 dE3 kI8 fR4 jU7 gT5 hY6 ;P? ,.½
3. Pr Ox La Ia Ka Me Us Ja Na Ye Ha Br Ur Ma He Mi
4. Qu Al Wh Sk Zo Ep Du Xe Cr Ri Fl To Gy Vo Ag Do
5. Ace Nun Cat Pun Tax You Fad Him Get Pin Car Nil
6. Sea Jim Wad Ink Vat Boy Gas Lop Wax Lip Arc Hop

Exercise 18

1. Area Lake Stab Kind Deaf John Face Hire Gain 23
2. Quad Pint Wait Omit Earl Idea Ream Unit Teak 45
3. Yank Zeal Male Xyst Nile Coke Back Vest Acts 67
4. Award Latin Stamp Knife Dance Joint Flour Heart
5. Brass Quart Pearl Watch Ocean Earth Index Ready
6. Uncle Total Young Cable Manor Vocal Naval Treat

*Reminders: set margin stops at 25 and 75 (Elite type) or 16 and 66 (Pica type);
little fingers to operate shift keys; shift key to be fully depressed and held during
the striking of the character key.*

Exercise 19

1. Bizet & Co offered us this page (6" x 8") for £9.

2. Ted's quotations are: 18/20p or 30/35p per kilo.

3. Please send, by the end of this week, a cheque for £247.

4. Colon (:) and semicolon (;) appear on the one key.

5. Their invoice was for 5 copies @ 65p, less 12½%. *

6. Will John send them another copy of this 70p book

Exercise 20

The following are among the 'Teach Yourself' subjects:-

ASTRONOMY – BIOLOGY – CHEMISTRY – MARKETING – MECHANICS

PHYSICS – ELECTRICITY – NAVIGATION – GEOLOGY – GEOMETRY

ELECTRONICS – SOCIOLOGY – MATHEMATICS – MUSIC – ALGEBRA

SPELLING – PHILOSOPHY – CALCULUS – JAPANESE – ECONOMICS

TRIGONOMETRY – PHOTOGRAPHY – LINGUISTICS – SELF DEFENCE

Reminders: set margin stops at 25 and 75 (Elite type) or 16 and 66 (Pica type); for Exercise 19 and at 22 and 27 (Elite type) or 14 and 69 (Pica type) for Exercise 20; use shift lock when underscoring in the third line; shift lock to be used for five lines of Exercise 20 and to be released for dash between each item.

Capitals are used for numbers with names of monarchs, chapter headings, acts in plays and books of the Bible, and for enumerating paragraphs when it is not convenient to use arabic numerals:

```
Elizabeth II   Chapter XX    Act I
```

Small letters are commonly used for numbering the preliminary pages of a book, and for enumerating sub-paragraphs or subsections, scenes in plays or chapters in the Bible:

```
page vi       Scene iii
I Corinthians iv, 2
```

A letter placed before one of greater value indicates that the first is deducted from the second to find the sum (XL = 40), and a letter placed after one of greater value indicates that both are added to find the sum (LX = 60).

A line placed over any symbol indicates that its value is multiplied by 1000.

Roman numerals should be lined up underneath each other, either to the right or left.

Combination characters and special signs

When not provided on the keyboard, a number of characters can be made by using two keys. Some single keys normally having a different purpose may be used for special signs.

Where two characters are required, one can be typed with or over another by holding down the space bar while the two characters are struck in succession, or by striking one of the two signs and then, after backspacing, striking the second sign over the first. For upper-case characters the shift key should be locked in position and the space bar held while the keys are struck.

For some of these combination signs it will be necessary to use the variable line spacer (or interliner) to allow the characters to be raised or lowered slightly above or below the line of writing. Where half-line spacing is provided on the typewriter, this will often provide the necessary line variation. A decimal point should not be raised above the line.

The following list of combination characters and signs is arranged in alphabetical order and should be practised even if the typewriter being used has some of them.

Asterisk	*	Small **x** and hyphen raised half a space above the line of writing
Brace	(or) ( )	Opening or closing brackets
Caret	⌐	Oblique stroke and underscore
Cent	¢	Small **c** and oblique stroke
Dagger	†	Capital **I** and hyphen raised half a space above the line of writing
Dash	-	Hyphen preceded and followed by one space
Decimal point	3.5	Full stop on the line
Degrees	60°	Small **o** raised and close up to figure
Diaeresis	ü	Double quotes " over letter
Ditto	"	Double quotes
Division	÷	Colon : and hyphen -
Dollar	$	Capital **S** over oblique stroke /
Double dagger	‡	Two capital **I**'s
Equals sign	=	Hyphen and slightly raised hyphen
Exclamation mark	!	Apostrophe and full stop
Feet	12'	Apostrophe after figure
Fraction	61/16	Oblique stroke
Inches	9"	Double quotes " after figure
Minus	121 - 3	Hyphen preceded and followed by one space
Minutes	18'	Apostrophe after figure
Multiplication	4 x 5	Small **x** preceded and followed by one space
Seconds	30"	Double quotes " after figure
Section mark	§	Small **s** over small **s** or capital **S** over capital **S**
Square bracket	[ ]	Oblique stroke and underscore

9

Copying Practice

There has been graded practice on all four rows of the machine with the object of attaining keyboard mastery, but a good deal of supplementary copying practice will be necessary to complete that mastery. The sense of location will by now be fairly well developed, but regular daily copying practice will produce a noticeable improvement in accuracy and speed.

Even margins

The setting of the stop for the left-hand margin ensures evenness throughout, but the same perfection cannot be secured for the right-hand margin of typewritten work unless a machine with a justifying capability is being used.

In the earlier sections the exercises were arranged so that the right-hand margin finished at the same point of the scale, but normally this uniformity cannot be obtained. Evenness can, however, be achieved to a reasonable extent by using the hyphen for the division of words, although it should not be overdone. When used, the hyphen should be inserted at the end and not at the beginning of a line.

Division of words

General guidelines for the division of words are given below:

1   A word of one syllable or its plural should not be divided.
2   A word should not be divided so that only two letters remain at the end of a line or are carried forward to the next line.

3 A hyphenated word should only be divided at the existing hyphen.

4 Proper names and abbreviations should not be divided.

5 Dates should not be divided.

6 Serial numbers should not be divided.

7 A person's initials should not be separated from the surname – the forename should follow the title and may be separated in this instance from the surname.

8 A divided word should not end a paragraph or page.

9 A word should not be divided in such a way that pronunciation of either half is affected.

10 Words containing double consonants may usually be divided between those consonants.

11 Words containing three consecutive consonants may be divided after the first consonant.

12 Compound words may be divided at point of juncture.

13 A word may be divided after a prefix or before a suffix, provided that a two-letter division does not result.

14 Sums of money should not be divided.

15 If in doubt as to the correct point of division, do not divide.

When the bell gives warning of the approach of the end of the line of writing (usually six or eight spaces), a decision has to be made regarding the division of the word.

Line spacing

Standard typewriters generally provide for three depths of spacing between lines—*single-line spacing* (no space between the lines), *double-line spacing* (a depth of one blank line between each line of typewriting) and *treble-line spacing* (a depth of two line spaces between each line of typewriting). These three forms are shown in Exercise 21, and when typing this the line space gauge should be properly adjusted for each depth of space and the line space lever operated to its fullest extent when returning the carriage to the right of the machine. The underscoring of the three items in the exercise will require the use of the shift lock. Here, the underscore is used for emphasis, and other uses for it are referred to on page 122.

Exercise 21

Set margin stops at 30 and 66 (Elite type) and 25 and 60 (Pica type);

Single-line spacing is generally
used for long letters, invoices,
tabular statements, poetry,
synopses, footnotes, minutes and
lengthy documents. Double-line
spacing is always used between
paragraphs, except between blocked
paragraphs when double spacing is
used, when it is necessary to turn
up twice.

Double-line spacing is used for

short letters, lecture notes,

literary work, essays, sermons,

legal documents, dialogue in plays

and copy intended for the printer.

Treble-line spacing is used for

drafts, and for literary and legal

work which may need revision.

Spacing after punctuation signs

The method of spacing recommended and adopted in the examples in this book is one space after a comma, colon or semicolon and two spaces after the full stop at the end of a sentence, and after the exclamation mark and interrogation mark. When the hyphen is used for the dash sign there should be a space both before and after the dash, and when the quotation marks (or inverted commas) and parentheses (or brackets) are typed they should not be separated by any space from the words they enclose. Other methods of spacing are recognised, but, whichever style is decided upon, there must be consistency throughout the work. If for example, three spaces are preferred after the full stop, this break should be made after every sentence in a typescript.

Copying exercises

There is no need for the copying practice to be limited to the exercises given here. A section of any book, periodical or newspaper can be used for this purpose.

Practice material on one-line sentences is contained in Exercises 22 and 23, and each sentence should be copied separately several times. In this way it will be possible to increase the copying speed.

There are paragraphs of varying length in Exercises 24 to 30. In the first place, the exercise should not be taken as a whole but each individual paragraph should be typed repeatedly until an increase in the speed is apparent. Some miscellaneous characters are included in Exercise 31.

The names of the writers of the passages in Exercise 28 are underscored, and in typewriting the underscore (which should be struck lightly) is used to indicate that the words underlined would appear in italics in ordinary printed matter. The underscore is also used for emphasising important words, for display work, for foreign words and phrases not anglicised, for scientific terms and for authorities at the end of quotations or notes.

When underscoring, the carriage should not be returned by means of the line space lever but should be pushed back by the platen knob until the writing point appears immediately under the first letter of the word to be underlined. The underscore should never commence or extend under a punctuation mark preceding or following the word or words to be emphasised.

Where there is difficulty in typing any particular word, that word should be repeatedly typed until the letter combination can be copied at a fair rate of speed.

Do not be content with copying the complete exercises once only; they should be copied several times, even if 100 per cent accuracy has been achieved at the first attempt. Repetition of any action facilitates its performance. An effort should be made to increase slightly the speed of operation at each successive attempt. And, here again, a previous direction is emphasised – *do not sacrifice accuracy to speed.*

Exercise 22

To get satisfactory work clean your machines every day.

They have arranged to forward this book by parcel post.

See a specialist before you agree to another operation.

We have now seen a full account of the new competition.

If they miss this train they will have an hour to wait.

Type four letters on company paper and post them today.

They had another book dealing with short story writing.

He had gone before we were able to check the signature.

Many of the men were not able to work during last week.

Most people would agree with their view on the subject.

Set margin stops at 22 and 77 (Elite type); 15 and 70 (Pica type)

Exercise 23

A perfect copy is possible when you are a touch typist.
I am pleased to acknowledge the good work done by them.
We are having another machine at the end of next month.
They have taken the house and will be moving in August.
The retail price of butter will be increased next week.
Please co-operate with him as he is having a busy time.
If we add a form it will make a difference to the book.
There is now no doubt about the truth of their remarks.
It will be a pleasure for me to represent this company.
Please send him details of the "Teach Yourself" Series.

Set margin stops at 22 and 77 (Elite type); 15 and 70 (pica type)

Exercise 24

An agenda is a list showing the order and
nature of the business to be transacted at a
meeting. Its preparation is usually entrusted
to the secretary or to the person responsible
for convening the meeting.

Of all the various forms of written communication used in organisations the letter is by
far the most common. It provides an essential
link between the executives and departments of
an organisation and the many external customers, associates and suppliers who are
necessary to the successful running of either
a business or government department.

Public companies represent the largest type
of business organisation other than those
owned by the government. They are composed
of shareholders who are at liberty to sell their
shares publicly without the consent of their
fellow shareholders.

In general, a director is one who has the chief
management of a scheme, design or undertaking.
More particularly, he is one of a number of
persons chosen by a majority of the shareholders
to conduct the affairs of a company.

Exercise 25

Book-keeping is the technique of keeping
accounts, and recording in a regular, concise
and accurate manner the financial transactions
of a firm in order to show the financial position
at any time.

Dividend is the proportion of profit distributed
to the shareholders as a reward for investing
in the company. It is expressed either as an
amount per share or as a percentage of the
nominal value of each share.

An overdraft is the amount of cash which a
banker allows his customer to draw out of his
bank account in excess of the total balance in
the customer's account.

An audit is an official examination of the
accounts of a firm to ensure that they are kept
in an accurate manner. Laws require the
regular inspection of accounting records by
auditors.

The Bank of England was suggested by
William Paterson, a Scotsman, and it received
its charter of incorporation in the year 1694.
It was constituted as a joint-stock company
with a capital of £1 200 000, that sum being
lent at interest to the Government of the day.

Exercise 26

An actuary is a person skilled in the calculation
of the value of life annuities and insurances
from mortality tables and upon mathematical
principles, and in the preparation of reports,
etc., in connection with insurance matters
generally.

The Baltic Mercantile and Shipping Exchange
(commonly known as The Baltic) is an association of merchants, shipowners, brokers and
various allied trades connected with grain, oil
oil-seed, timber, coal, etc.

A bill of lading is an acknowledgment of the
shipment of goods which also contains the terms
and conditions agreed upon as to their carriage.
It is not necessarily the contract of carriage
itself, though it is excellent evidence of it.

A legal day is the whole of the day, continuing
up to midnight. When there is an obligation to
do a certain thing by a fixed day, the whole day
must pass before there can be default. For
example, if rent is payable on a quarter day,
it is not in arrear until the day following.

Shipbrokers are agents - persons or firms -
in a seaport appointed by shipowners to carry
out and perform all the necessary transactions
connected with the business of their vessels
while they are in harbour, such as entering
and clearing the vessels, collecting freight, etc.

Exercise 27

Truth is always consistent with itself, and
needs nothing to help it out. It is always near
at hand, and sits upon our lips, and is ready
to drop out before we are aware; whereas a
lie is troublesome, and sets a man's invention
upon the rack, and one trick needs a great
many more to make it good.

Shirking duty, or running away from the things
that we feel we ought to do, has a peculiarly
demoralising effect on one's high purpose of
right. Our judgment of what our duty is may
be a mistaken one, but there is something im-
perious about the call of duty that makes the
slighting of it a very serious matter indeed.

We shall never be sorry afterwards for thinking
twice before we speak, for counting the cost
before entering upon any new course, for
sleeping over stings and injuries before saying
or doing anything in answer, or for carefully
considering any business scheme presented to
us before putting money or name into it.

A public speaker is a mental guide. He leads
his audience, step by step, through a succession
of ideas, to a logical conclusion. If he is not
prepared; if each of these steps or ideas is not
clearly defined; if his thoughts are but vaguely
conceived; if the bearing of the individual
thoughts upon the conclusion is not clear, confusion follows.

Exercise 28

When a great man, who has engrossed our
thoughts, our conjectures, our homage, dies,
a gap seems suddenly left in the world; a wheel
in the mechanism of our own being appears
abruptly stilled; a portion of ourselves, and not
our worst portion - for how many pure, high,
generous sentiments it contains! - dies with
him. - Lord Lytton.

It is idleness that creates impossibilities; and,
where men care not to do a thing, they shelter
themselves under a persuasion that it cannot be
done.   The shortest and the surest way to prove
a work possible is strenuously to set about it.
- Robert South.

The only freedom which deserves the name is
that of pursuing our own good in our own way,
so long as we do not attempt to deprive others
of theirs, or impede their efforts to obtain it.
Each is the proper guardian of his own health,
whether bodily or mental and spiritual.
- John Stuart Mill.

With malice towards none; with charity for all;
with firmness in the right, as God gives us to
see the right, let us strive on to finish the
work we are in; to bind up the nation's wounds;
to care for him who shall have borne the battle,
and for his widow, and his orphan - to do all
which may achieve and cherish a just and a
lasting peace among ourselves, and with all
nations. - Abraham Lincoln.

Exercise 29

Efficient filing depends on the storage of letters
and other documents to preserve them from
dirt and damage and their arrangement according to some plan, so that any letter or document can afterwards be obtained quickly.   The
plan to be followed must be worked out in
sufficient detail to provide an exact place for
every letter or document.   Ease of reference
is quite as important as preservation from
damage.

Every caller at a business organisation is,
as a member of the public, a potential buyer
of goods or services, even if he has come to
sell.   His good will is valuable, no matter
who he is, and its cultivation is in the hands
of the receptionist.   A naturally good receptionist is as rare as the naturally good hostess,
and any girl who finds that, through shyness
or inexperience, she is unable to cope should
learn the part of the receptionist as if it were
a part in a play.

On the telephone the voice is an important
factor and has to stand on its own merits,
deprived of all assistance from gesture and
facial expression.   Many people who appear
gracious and lucid in an ordinary conversation
seem surly and confused on the telephone.   All
people using the telephone should study the
faults they encounter at the other end of the
line and strive to eliminate all of them at their
end.

Exercise 30

For folding a large number of letters, statements, leaflets, etc. , a folding machine is
available. The papers are laid in packets on
the feeding ledge of the machine, which is
electrically driven and automatically fed, and
folding proceeds at the rate of approximately
6000 an hour. Many sizes of folds may be
arranged by adjusting the machine.

The production of a business letter is very
much the result of teamwork. First and
foremost a graphics designer settles upon
a suitable design for the organisation's letterhead. Then an office manager has to decide
upon the colour and quality of the paper on
which the letterhead will be printed. Many
firms take a great deal of trouble over
choosing the colours of paper and letterhead
designs, since they know that a good combination will go a long way towards persuading
the receiver to accept the letter's message.

You will learn much of your spelling by keeping your eyes open as you go along the streets,
and by careful observation when reading your
books or newspapers. There are also many
attractive advertisements and posters which
will help in teaching you how to spell. Whenever you see a word, the spelling of which
causes difficulty, look closely at it to obtain
a correct mental picture. This method is
more valuable than trying to remember a
number of spelling rules and their exceptions.

Exercise 31

The interrogation mark (?) is used when a
direct question is asked; an example is: What
is the price of Jack's book on Zoology?

The signs & (and) and @ (at) should never be
used in the body of a document as a substitute
for the word or words. The ampersand (&)
may only be used in names of companies,
street numbers and abbreviations, and the
@ sign may only be used in accounts, invoices,
price lists or quotations. The per cent sign
% should only be used when immediately following an arabic numeral.

10

Punctuation

Correct punctuation is essential for the production of good typewritten work and should be studied carefully. The examples given below show some of the chief uses of the various punctuation marks, which are arranged in alphabetical order. The portions in typewriter type should be copied several times.

Apostrophe (')
The main functions of the apostrophe are to indicate ownership, contraction or omission, and the formation of plurals of letters and figures. It is represented on the typewriter keyboard by the single quotation mark.

The possessive singular is indicated by adding 's:

```
The typist's chair.
Mr Ward's typewriter.
Mr Spring's desk.
Anderson's car.
```

By adding the apostrophe only, the possessive plural is indicated:

```
Only seven days' notice is required.
Six months' leave was granted.
```

When the plural form does not end in s, 's is added to form the possessive, as in *men's clothes*, *children's holidays*.

Possessive *pronouns* do not require the apostrophe:

```
This is ours.  Where is yours?
The dog wagged its tail.
Theirs is in the corner.
She has his and hers.
```

An apostrophe indicates the omission of a letter or letters:

```
Don't    it's    can't
```

In the case of plural formation of abbreviations, letters and figures, the 's is added:

```
There were many MP's.
You don't sound your t's.
Two 2's
```

Capitals

Names of persons, months, days, places and book titles are written with an initial capital letter:

```
John Brown      England     New York
January         Tuesday
'Business Man's Guide'
```

Adjectives derived from proper names should be similarly treated:

```
Indian    French Revolution
```

although there are some exceptions:

```
india rubber    french windows
```

Colon (:)

The colon, although separating parts of a compound sentence, indicates continuity of thought:

```
Be careful how you act: actions speak
louder than words.
```

A longer pause is denoted by the colon rather than by the semicolon.

Important uses of the colon are to introduce quotations, lists, summaries and explanations:

```
The following books are recommended:
'Teach Yourself Mathematics', 'English
for Business', 'The Pitman Dictionary
of English and Shorthand'.
```

The lists may be run on or be typed in column form.

Comma (,)

The comma denotes the shortest pause or break in continuity:

```
They live in houses, not in huts.
```

A short sentence of simple construction does not require commas:

```
I shall go there tomorrow.
```

Between two long phrases joined by "and", the comma is often inserted:

```
We thank you for your letter, and
have pleasure in accepting the
offer.
```

Dash (−)

The dash may be used to indicate a break in a sentence. It is also used to separate items, for example the contents of chapters of a book, and precedes definitions, explanations and illustrations:

```
There are two kinds of spacing in
typewriting - character spacing and
line spacing.
```

When typing the dash leave one space before and after.

Emphasis

The underscore can be used to emphasise a particular expression:

```
We shall require copies not later
than Wednesday next.
```

Exclamation, note of (!)

An exclamation mark denotes an expression of wish or emotion:

```
Good luck!        Delightful!
```

Full stop or period (.)

This mark is used to note the end of a complete sentence that is neither a question nor an exclamation:

```
Please reply to our previous letter.
```

The full stop is used as a decimal point:

```
125.65          £4.20
```

After initials denoting forenames the full stop is inserted, provided that open punctuation (see page 75) is not being employed.

Three full stops (ellipses) are used to indicate the omission of words:

```
'Go to the shop ... and I'll wait for you.'
```

Leader lines, which are used to guide the eye from one column to another, are made by using the full stop. The dots are continuous, with one space between the last preceding character and the first dot:

```
10 copies .................... 15p
```

The use of the full stop after general abbreviations and contractions is covered under *Open and closed punctuation* on page 75.

Hyphen (-)
This may show the relationship of two words forming a compound word:

```
Half-length       Self-contained
```

The hyphen is also used to mark division of a word at the end of the line of writing, the remainder being carried to the beginning of the next line.

Nowadays, the tendency is to use the hyphen as seldom as possible, and many words which were formerly hyphenated (for example, co-operate) are now written as one word (cooperate).

Interrogation, note of (?)
This is used after a direct question:

```
What is the price of the Portable?
```

A question mark is not necessary when an order is given in the form of a question:

```
Will you kindly let us have the
information as soon as possible.
```

Parenthesis ( )
This is used to enclose subsidiary words, clauses or sentences to

explain the leading idea of the sentence:

```
The order to which you refer (No 16)
has now been completed.

Tinted typewriting papers (usually
of cheaper qualities) are used chiefly
for carbon copies.
```

Square brackets – [ ] – are used to make further enclosure within a parenthesis, and also in legal work.

Parentheses should be used sparingly, to avoid awkward sentences.

Quotation marks (' ' or " ")

Quotation marks are used to enclose words exactly as quoted:

```
I wish,' he said. 'to express my gratitude.
```

The quotation mark should not be placed at the beginning of every line of a quoted paragraph, only before the first word of each paragraph and at the end of the complete quotation.

The choice of single or double quotation marks is optional, but the style adopted should be used consistently. When a citation occurs within a citation, the alternative form should be used to avoid confusion.

Semicolon (;)

The use of the semicolon indicates a pause in a sentence where the second clause is too closely linked to the first to justify complete separation:

```
There has been more than one
postponement; frequent con-
sultations have taken place.
```

This mark is also used between clauses of compound sentences:

```
The girls attended the lectures;
the boys were not interested.
```

Open and closed punctuation

The method of typewriting which uses a minimum of punctuation is
known as open punctuation. This speeds up and simplifies the typist's
work, and is most apparent in the omission of full stops after
abbreviations. The following comparisons show how punctuation
marks may be omitted without any loss of clarity.

Open punctuation

```
We shall expect you at 9 am on Thursday.
Mr J T Smith BSc FRSA
Harry works in the USA.
Please check in at 1500 hrs on Sunday.
Sell all the furniture, ie the tables
  and chairs.
This can be paid at any SWEB shop.
PS  Greece is a member of the EEC.
HRH The Princess of Wales.
Bring all your old toys, etc, to the sale.
```

Closed punctuation

```
We shall expect you at 9 a.m. on Thursday.
Mr. J. T. Smith, B.Sc., F.R.S.A.
Harry works in the U.S.A.
Please check in at 1500 hrs. on Sunday.
Sell all the furniture, i.e. the tables
  and chairs.
This can be paid at any S.W.E.B. shop.
P.S.  Greece is a member of the E.E.C.
H.R.H. The Princess of Wales.
Bring all your old toys, etc., to the
  sale.
```

Since open punctuation is now widely accepted, most of the typed
examples in the book will follow this style. Whichever method is
chosen, however, it is important to show consistency within a single
piece of work.

11

Deciphering Manuscript –
Correction Signs

So far, the copying practice has been from typewritten examples or printed matter, but most typists need to be able to decipher manuscript.

Before starting to prepare a typescript from a handwritten original the typist should read a fairly lengthy section in order to get to know the writer's style. When there is any difficulty in deciphering a word, leave a space as it may be possible to fill in the correct word later.

Abbreviations

Abbreviations may be used by the originator, and these should always be typed in full in the final copy. Some examples are:

Abbreviation	*Word(s)*
abt	about
aftn	afternoon
asap	as soon as possible
asst	assistant
bn	been
mtg	meeting
plse	please
shd	should
wk(s)	week(s)
wh	which
wd	would
Yrs ffy	Yours faithfully

Drafts are generally typed in double-line spacing, although treble-line spacing is the usual practice for legal documents, which often undergo extensive revision by each party before being prepared for signature.

Correction signs

Manuscript or typescript drafts often contain marginal notes or interlineations. The typist should be able to follow these correctly and also be aware of the correction signs in common use. These are given in the table below:

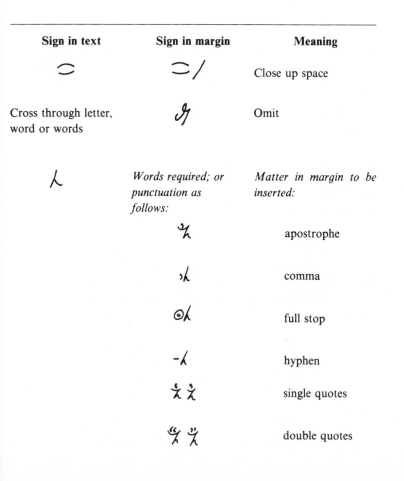

Sign in text	Sign in margin	Meaning
⌒	⌒/	Close up space
Cross through letter, word or words		Omit
⋏	*Words required; or punctuation as follows:*	*Matter in margin to be inserted:*
		apostrophe
		comma
		full stop
		hyphen
		single quotes
		double quotes

Underline or cross through letter(s) to be altered	*lc*	Lower case – small letters
⌈ or ∥	*NP or para*	New paragraph
⌒	*run on*	Do not begin a new paragraph
/	#	insert space
– – – – – –	*stet*	Do not omit parts struck out and dotted underneath
⌐⌐⌐	*trs*	Reverse the order
Underline or cross through letter(s) to be altered	*uc*	Upper case – capital letters

Exercises 32 to 35 contain amendments and correction signs, while Exercises 36 and 37 give the learner an opportunity to decipher difficult handwriting. Use double-line spacing and block paragraphs for these exercises (remembering to turn up twice between paragraphs), then check with the keys on pages 176–81.

Exercise 32

The question of the original home of the tea
plant is by no means settled, the point at
issue being whether~~, after all,~~ the true home   S/
of the plant is in China or Assam. Because
the tea plant attains extraordinary luxuriance
in Assam, it could be argued that this is its
natural home. However, it has been noticed
that plants introduced into new countries have
lc.   flourished as well as <u>N</u>ative plants. [A Japan- NP
ese legend ascribes to China the honour of being
the home of the tea plant and there are certain
references to the plant in the writings of a
Chinese author who lived about 2,700 BC.   run on

A Chinese commentator on this ancient author͵
calls attention to the mention of the plant
and adds that a beverage could be obtained
from the leaves by adding hot water. It
\#   appears that the plant was used entirely as a
medicine until AD 550 when it became a popular
beverage.

, writing in the fourth
century BC,

(Key on page 176)

Exercise 33

Originally the work of professional accountants
trs was chiefly confined to the checking of arithmetical accuracy of the detailed records of
transactoins in books on account, the agreement f/
uc of the trial Balance, and the preparation of
-/ accounts in fact, to what may be described as
y/y accountancy work but nowadays the all important j/-/
part of a professional accountants work is that y
of auditing. The difference between account- NP
ancy and auditing is not clearly understood by
many business men, it being thought that if
accounts are prepared by a professional accountant he necessarily guarantees their accuracy.
,/ This, however is far from being the case. run on

an/ If accountant is instructed merely to prepare
accounts from a set of books, he would be acting
simply as an expert accountant, and not in any
lc way as an Auditor.

(Key on page 177)

Exercise 34

The effect that colour has on us, is being
looked at more and more closely.

(and our feelings)

nn on

In america it was found that output in a
factory went up 3(%) when rest areas were
painted a horrible bright green because staff
couldn't bear to stay too long. Workmen
considered some big dark boxes too heavy to
haul until they were painted a lighter colour.
[yellow is believed to be happy and free ;
Blue calming and cool, giving a feeling of
security and peace / orange outgoing and warm;
Red is exciting to some people but can be
oppressive as well. It has the most direct
impact on the senses and can make people
argue so beware of painting a room in your
home red. Violet can cause one to hesitate.
Which colour takes the helm — the aggressive
red or the calmer blue ?

with its make-up
of blue and red

uc
per cent

NP
lc.
⊙h

ph

(Key on page 178)

Exercise 35

To write is not necessarily to
communicate with another mind.
writing is primarily expression - and
whoever has made ~~private~~ use of it   ∅
to record what he has felt and
thought and done ⌐ will know already   *, or as*
that such exercises are in themselves   *a means of*
simply rewording. ⌐   *meditation,*

                                           run on

⌐ He will know also that the practice of
writing to oneself is invaluable.
[What are the main advantages of   *NP*
written expression? as against thinking   *uc*
in the head ⌐? the written word gives   ∅
a fixed form to the underlying thought
it expresses. ~~and so enables~~ the writer   *∅ uc*
~~to⌐ judge whether the thought itself   *can then ⌐*
is of value and whether its expression
is adequate.

, which is more than
likely to be ~~vague~~
~~fragmentary,~~

(Key on page 179)

Exercise 36

Mass production is the name given to a method of manufacture in which one standard pattern takes the place of a variety of shapes and sizes. The principle is not new, and its advantages have been known in industry for a very long time. During the last few decades, however, a number of manufacturers have carried the method to its logical conclusion, which is: one kind of article only produced in a single factory. The advantages claimed for the mass production method are many. Chief among them is the possibility of adjusting the operations of manufacture so that there may be the completest economy in man- and machine power in every part of the work. The best known example of mass production is the motor car, an article which is complex and made of many parts. The principle adopted is that of a series of factories side by side in each of which a different part is made. Those parts pass on in continuous streams and on completion pass in to an assembly shop. Here the cars are gradually built up from the beginning to the end at an almost incredible rate of speed. From end to end the great saving of thought, time, and labour arises from the absolute similarity of one car to all others of the same class. Every worker repeats ad infinitum the operation that falls to him, till not a movement is wasted or a fraction of time is lost.

(Key on page 180)

Exercise 37

Libel is a term which in popular use includes any statement of a defamatory character made by one person of another. Technically, however, it includes any statements in writing or other more or less permanent record. Legally, spoken words are termed slander, and from the point of view of the person complaining the distinction is important. In the case of slander it is usually necessary to prove that as a result of words spoken the party claiming to be injured has suffered special damage, whilst in libel such proof is not necessary. Even in slander words imputing unfitness, dishonesty or incompetence in business or tending to prejudice a man in his public calling are actionable without proof of special damage. Even a public company may bring an action when defamation amounts to impeachment of its conduct of business.

Words spoken or written may on the face of them be innocent but they may have a hidden meaning understood by others. In such case the libel is by innuendo.

Fair comment on matters of public interest may be a justification of defamatory statements, and if the comment is fair and reasonable there is no libel. The standard of what is fair is not fixed but if the motive is pure the statement is generally justified, and the matter is a question of fact for the jury. Another justification is that the words spoken or written are true. This is a defence which must be proved to the hilt or the plea itself will aggravate the offence.

(Key on page 181)

12

Business Letters and Envelope Addressing

The letter is by far the most common form of written communication used by organisations, and these letters will convey their messages more effectively if they are attractively produced.

The chief characteristics of a good letter are clearness, accuracy, brevity and courtesy. There are various components of a business letter, and in the paragraphs that follow each portion is dealt with.

Sizes of letter paper
The standard size is A4 (210 mm × 297 mm; $8\frac{1}{4}$ in × $11\frac{3}{4}$ in). For very short letters and private correspondence, A5 (210 mm × 148 mm; $5\frac{7}{8}$ in × $8\frac{1}{4}$ in) is used.

Letter headings
These headings are generally the product of the graphics designer and printer, and are carefully prepared since they play an important part in projecting the desired corporate image. The details given in the letter heading include, in bold display type, the name and business of the firm, the company's registered address from which that business is conducted, company number, telephone and telex numbers, telegraphic address, etc. For private correspondence the letter paper usually contains the address and telephone number.

Width of margins
Margin widths are governed largely by individual preference and the length of the letter, and the margin stops should be set before commencing work. A minimum left margin of 25 mm (1 in) is

generally recommended for A4 paper, however, with a slightly narrower margin for A5. Modern practice is to allow even left and right margins to secure a centred effect on the paper, in much the same way as the printed page of a book.

Insertion of date
The order recommended is day, month (spelled out in full) and year typed on one line, as:

```
17 April 19-- or 17th April, 19--
```

Commence the date at the left-hand margin point when adopting the fully blocked style, and let it finish flush with the right-hand margin when using the indented or semi-blocked style of layout.

Reference initials
In business correspondence these references usually consist of the initials of the dictator and the typist, as **DF/OH** or **DF/oh**. Alternatively, a departmental number may be used, as **SALES/916**. If a place has not been allotted for these details in the printed letter heading, they can be placed at the left-hand margin, as shown in the examples on pages 93 and 100. Sometimes the initials are inserted at the end of the letter. When replying to a correspondent, do not forget to include his reference. It will be helpful to him in dealing with the letter – that is the reason for its insertion.

Attention line
When instructions are given that correspondence must be addressed to a firm and not to individuals, it is common practice to insert an attention line reading:

FOR THE ATTENTION OF MR J HARMAN

two line spaces below the inside address (see page 100).
    For the layout of an attention line on an envelope, see page 105.

Inside name and address
The name and address of the person or firm to whom the letter is being sent are in most cases placed at the beginning of the letter. Single-line spacing should be used, with all lines beginning at the left-

hand margin point. It is common practice to type the inside address in the same form as the envelope address (see page 104), with the post town in capital letters.

Every care should be taken to ensure that the name of the correspondent is given correctly.

Personal, private, confidential

When it is desired for a specific reason to restrict the reading of the letter to one particular person, the words giving the instruction should be typed, preferably in capitals, two line spaces above the inside address.

Salutation

The opening to a letter is termed the 'salutation', and the most common forms used include:

```
Dear Sir    Dear Mrs Jones    Dear Mr Smith
Dear Sirs   Dear Madam        Dear Ms Black
```

Type the salutation two or three line spaces below the inside address.

Subject heading

When a subject heading is required it should be typed two line spaces below the salutation and may be typed at the left-hand margin point or centred over the writing line. Unless the heading ends with an abbreviation, a full stop should not be inserted after it. A heading typed in lower case with initial capitals should preferably be underscored.

Body of letter

This contains the subject matter of the letter. It should commence two line spaces below the subject heading, or two line spaces below the salutation if there is no heading. Paragraphs may be blocked or indented according to the letter style. Single-line spacing with double-line spacing between paragraphs is preferable, but double-line spacing throughout is sometimes used for very short letters of one paragraph.

Do not use the ampersand (&) for 'and' in the body of the letter, unless reference is made to the name of a firm or street numbers are being quoted.

Insets
These are paragraphs that are displayed within the body of the letter. If the paragraphs are numbered or lettered, two or three spaces should be left after the number or letter or its closing bracket.

Inset paragraphs may be blocked, indented or 'hanging'. When the blocked method of layout is being used, 'inset' matter can begin at the left-hand margin. Otherwise, paragraphs should be indented equally from both margins. In 'hanging' paragraphs the first line overhangs the second and subsequent lines by two spaces.

Double-line spacing should always be used between the text and the inset material, and, unless the items are very short, between paragraphs in the portion inset.

Continuation sheets
These are necessary when a letter occupies more than one sheet of paper, and they should be of the same size and quality as the letter heading. Continuation sheets are not usually printed with the firm's letter heading. The details required on the continuation sheet are the page number, the date and the addressee.

When the fully blocked style of letter layout is used, the details are listed separately at the left-hand margin:

```
2
17April 19--
R Kelly Esq
```

With the indented method, the information is evenly displayed across one line with the page number in the centre:

```
R. Kelly, Esq.   (2)  17th April, 19--
```

Do not use a continuation sheet for only two lines. A readjustment of margins may make it possible to type the letter on one sheet.

Complimentary close

This is typed two line spaces below the final paragraph of the letter and should begin at the left-hand margin point or the middle of the line of writing. Those most used are:

```
Yours sincerely  Yours truly
     Yours faithfully
```

The form of complimentary close should match the salutation – 'Yours faithfully' with 'Dear Sir' but 'Yours sincerely' with 'Dear Mr Smith'.

Name of the firm or company

Capital letters are used if the name of the company follows the complimentary close, and the letter may be signed by a member of the staff who acts as an agent.

The name of the company may be prefaced by the word 'for'. The abbreviated form of *per procurationem* – **per pro**. or **p. p.** – is also used.

The signature

This will be handwritten, and, when the designation of the writer is placed after the complimentary close, a minimum of five line spaces should be left for the insertion of the signature. The designation should be typed at the left-hand margin point, or be centred under, or commence at the same point as, the complimentary close when the indented or semi-blocked style of layout is employed.

Enclosures

The indication of enclosures to a letter is given by typing the abbreviated form **Enc** or **2 Encs** in the space that may be provided for this information or at the bottom left-hand corner of the letter. (If there is room, **Enc** should be typed two or three line spaces below the designation.) Labels are sometimes affixed to the letter and a duplicate placed on the enclosure.

Another method of showing enclosures is to type three dots or hyphens in the margin on the same line as the reference to an enclosure.

Layout

On page 92 the layout for a fully blocked letter is given in diagrammatic form, together with a key to the sections, and on page 93 is an example of an open-punctuated fully blocked letter, with subject heading. This is the style most emphasised in this book, although it should be stressed that employers may have personal preferences with regard to layout and punctuation which should be followed.

Carbon copying

For business transactions it is desirable to have a record of documents despatched, and there are various methods of copying letters, etc. That most popular is the carbon-paper method; the copies are made at the same time as the original. The number of copies that can be secured by this means will depend upon the typewriter used and the quality of the typewriting paper.

Normally carbon paper can be obtained in a variety of sizes and colours, and single-sided carbons (coated on one side) are mostly used.

In preparing to take carbon copies, the first sheet should be placed face downwards on the table. On this a sheet of carbon paper should be placed, with the coated surface upwards; then another sheet of paper, another carbon and so on for the required number. See that the carbon sheets are in correct position so that all the original appears on the copies.

When the sheets are inserted in the machine, care should be taken to see that the coated side of the sheet faces the cylinder, and the pressure of the feed rolls should be released by depressing the paper release lever, particularly when there are several sheets. The pressure can be restored when the top edges of the sheets have passed the feed rolls. This pressure should also be released when the sheets are withdrawn from the machine.

It is usual to identify the recipient of a carbon copy on the original, by typing the name on the same line as the letters **cc**. Sometimes, however, a *blind carbon copy* (bcc) may be required – perhaps for a colleague, for information – in which case the letters **bcc** and the recipient's name or designation are typed on the carbon(s) only, and not on the original.

Corrections on carbon copies

One method of correction is to place a small piece of paper between each carbon and its copy at the point where the erasure is to be made. First, make the erasure on the top copy; next lift the first carbon and remove the small piece of paper and erase the error from the carbon copy; then lift the second carbon and follow the same procedure until all the copies have been dealt with. Before typing the correction all the pieces of paper must be removed.

Carbon economy

Wastage of carbon sheets can be avodied by reversing them immediately there is sign of wear, the bottom carbon being placed at the top for subsequent copies. When one particular area has been in fairly constant use, the remainder may be practically untouched. Alternatively, cut away a small portion of the top edge so that, when the trimmed edge is placed at the top of the paper, an additional unused surface becomes available.

Exercises

Copy the letter on page 93 on A5 portrait (shorter side at top), then type Exercises 38 to 43, using the same style. Insert fictitious references and the date.

PRINTED HEADING

(1) . . . .

(2) . . . .

(3) . . . .
. . . .
. . . .
. . . .

(4) . . . .

(5) . . . .

(6) . . . .
. . . .
. . . .

(6) . . . .
. . . .

(7) . . . .

(8) . . . .

(9) . . . .

(10) . . . .

(11) . . . .

(12) . . . .

The numbers refer to the following sections of the letter: (1) Reference; (2) Date; (3) Name and address of the addressee; (4) Salutation; (5) Subject heading; (6) Paragraphs in body of letter; (7) Complimentary close; (8) Firm name; (9) Signatory's name; (10) Signatory's designation; (11) Enclosure; (12) Carbon copy

Layout for a fully blocked letter

Example of an open-punctuated fully blocked style, with subject heading

```
Your ref EMD/AE
Our ref EJJ/EMH
(3)
10 May 19--
(3)
Messrs John Cross & Co
235-239 High Street
SHEFFIELD
S1 7TR
(3)
Dear Sirs
(2)
ROLLER BOOK BACKING MACHINE
(2)
We are contemplating the installation of one of
these machines, 325 mm wide, and shall be glad to
know what is your lowest price and when you can
deliver a machine.
(2)
For some years we have had one of your machines of
this size in constant use here, and it has always
given us great satisfaction.
(2)
We shall be glad to have a reply at your earliest
convenience.
(2)
Yours faithfully
MOORLANDS & JOHNSON LTD


(6)


E J Johnson
Director
```

Note:

1   The numbers between the parts of the letter show the number of lines to turn up.

2   Because this letter uses open punctuation, there are no punctuation marks above and below the body of the letter.

Exercise 38

(Reference)
(Today's date)

The Gen Man, Bridge Machinery Company.
Garner Road, Stockport, Cheshire SK5 6EP

Dear Sir

As you know, we are hvg a great deal of
trouble with the Crosfad machine which yr (CROSFORD)
installed last month. Our maintenance
engineer has followed yr suggestions, but the results
are still v. unsatisfactory. [In the circs, we   NP/
shall be pleased if you will arrange to
send yr expert ~~as soon as~~ poss. to inspect (this week
the machine and advise us.   if)

Yrs faithfully.

P L Jones
Manager

(Key on page 182)

Exercise 39

(Reference)
(Today's date)

The Gen Man,
Brick + Steel Limited
Palace Wharf
Edgware
ED7 3LT

Dear Sir Flats at main Avenue, Willesden
Youf are invited to tender for the erection
of a block of flats at the above location for the   uc
Housing Trust Ltd, and I shall be pleased
if you will let me know asap whether you
desire to tender, in order that quantities may
be sent to you. The drawings of the proposed
work may be inspected at in my office on
making an apptut. [Tenders are to be delivered   NP
to me within one month. Yrs ffy

(Key on page 183)

Exercise 40

(Reference)
(Today's date)

Mr John Andrews
Messrs Andrews & Son
14 - 16 Church Street
Liverpool
L1 3AA

Dear Mr Andrews
Thank you for your recent enquiry. We
are enc. our latest cat. and price list,
and are asking our rep to call on you
next week to discuss the best word
processor for your needs. [In the   NP
meantime, we shall be pleased if you
will give us additional partics. by
filling in the att. form and returning
it ~~as soon as possible~~ *at once* to this office   stet

Yrs sinc.   A Jones Sales Man.

Encs

(Key on page 184)

Exercise 41

(Reference)
(Today's date)

The Sales Manager, Climax Steel Co Limited,
209 - 211 Chesterfield Street, Sheffield S1 0SA

Dr Sir

We are sending herewith our Order No 608
for Steel Angles and Channels, which we
are urgently requiring in connection
with an imp contract. Delivery is of
extreme importance and we shd
like to hv the material in our Works
by next weekend if poss.

The bars to be supplied wd be of
ordinary commercial quality, and while
the quantity is large you will observe
that there only three sections involved.
In these circs. we hv no doubt you will
be able to meet our requirements in
regard to delivery.

immediately
Please let us know by return the
very best you can do for us.

Yrs ffy
R + S BUILDERS

A D Jones
Asst Man
Enc.

(Key on page 185)

Exercise 42

(Reference)

(Today's date)

Mr J W Webb, Chief Design Engineer, Messrs John
Smith & Company, 901 London Road, Maidstone,
MA5 6LR

Dear Mr Webb

Owing to ~~The~~ steady growth of our business ~~has made it~~
~~necessary to move~~ *we are moving* to larger premises in Main
Street, Slough, Bucks at the end of this month.
The site is a particularly good one, in the
heart of this industrial centre, within easy
london and reach of the M4 Motorway. The transport difficulties which we have experienced in the past
will now be reduced to a minimum, and early
deliveries ensured. [The new factory will be   *NP*
fully automated with a resulting increase in
both the quality and quantity of our output.

We trust that you will be patient with us during
trs this transitional period. Any delays should be
trs minimal only and we expect to ~~be in~~ full production again within five weeks. *λ achieve*

May we take this opportunity of expressing our
thanks for yr confidence in the past & we hope
that the improvements we shall introduce will
lead to even more business.

Yrs sinc
J Simpson
Gen Man

(Key on page 186)

Exercise 43

(Reference)
(Today's date)

The Gen Man, J. Finn & Company Limited,
534 Western Rd. Swindon, SN2 5DA

Dr Sir   We shld be pleased to assist you to the
best of our ability to replenish yr stock on
advantageous terms. [The enc illustrated cat   /NP
contains concise details of the many household
gds that we think wd interest you.

We hv just bn appointed agents for the mnfcrs of
a British-made oil heater which is both cheap &
satisfactory & yr special inquiry reaches us at the
right moment. The heater is obtainable in various
models at prices from £35.60 & has the following
special points.

2. The flame is easily adjustable to any reasonable
   height, giving greatly increased comfort.
3. With the patent burner any excess of oil is
   drained back into the tank, ensuring safety &
   complete elimination of smoke & smell.
4. The heater burns at full capacity for a cost of
   approx. 5p an hour
1. It gives a maximum heat of twice as much warmth
   as other heaters in its class.

If you will let us know yr requirements we will
instruct our rep to call on you.
Yrs ffy
T R Cockburn
Sales Man
Enc   *(Key on page 187)*

Your ref: WPH/EMJ
Our ref: ATN/MG   10 May, 19--

Messrs. H. Blakemore & Sons,
167 Wordsworth Road,
READING.
RG1 6DW

For the attention of Mr. John Harman

Dear Sirs,

We have your letter of yesterday's date, and are
prepared to grant you an agency for the sale of our
goods on the following terms:

(1) We will allow you a commission of 20 per
     cent off catalogue prices on all goods
     purchased by you or through your agency,
     and also a discount of 5 per cent on
     accounts paid within one month from date
     of invoice. You are, however, to forgo
     discount on accounts not paid within three
     months.

(2) We will undertake not to grant another
     agency in your district.

(3) We will furnish you with catalogues
     periodically, setting out particulars
     and prices, and bearing your name and
     address as district agents, together
     with leaflets with your name and address
     printed thereon.

(4) We will send goods to your premises
     packed and carriage paid.

If the above terms are satisfactory to you, we shall
be pleased to discuss the matter further.

                        Yours faithfully,
                        for J. ANDREW & CO. LTD.

                        A. T. Noakes

*Copy this letter on A4 paper and then type Exercise 44 on the following
page, using the same style. Note that the letter is fully punctuated.*

Exercise 44

(Reference)   (Today's date)

Mr. William Mortimore,
The Cedars,
Manor Crescent,
Harrogate
NA7 9PQ

Dear ~~Sir~~, Mr. M

We are v glad that you hv written to
us to query some of the items on the
bill that we sent to you, since we
always urge customers ~~to write~~ to   ᵒᶠ
let us know when they do not feel
satisfied. [With regard to the oil wh   NP
you state is v much clearer than before,
we wd mention th you agreed a better
grade of oil would conserve the engine
power for a longer period, + you
authorized us to supply you with a more
expensive brand. [Concerning the ~~service~~ ˡᵃᵇᵒᵘʳ   NP
charge of £10.00 for repair to the front
bumper, this was undertaken at the ~~order~~ ʳᵉqᵘᵉˢᵗ
of yr son.

On any matter ∧

We regret that we are unable to reduce
the charge for the materials, as this
was previously agreed upon as being
reasonable.

                    Yours ~~faithfully~~, sincerely

          P.J. Jones,
          Service Manager.

(Key on page 188)

Ref: AD/DW   24 March, 19--

Messrs. Plummer & Co.,
841 Market Street,
ST. ALBANS.
AL5 6BZ

Dear Sirs,

                    New Price List

        We shall be grateful if you will send us a
quotation for producing 50,000 copies of our price
list in accordance with the attached specifications.

        We enclose a copy of the one previously
issued, which was produced for us by another firm
of printers, and we shall be glad if you will follow
this for general style.

        We wish to have this price list ready for
distribution at the earliest possible moment, and
shall appreciate anything you can do to help us.

                    Yours faithfully,
            for WHITEHEAD & SAUNDERS LTD,

                    Manager

Enc.

Copy this letter on A5 paper and then type Exercise 45, using the same style.

Exercise 45

(Reference)   (Today's date)

Messrs. Benham & Brown,
417 Selwyn Road, London, E13 0PY

Dear Sirs,
        We confirm our conversation on
the telephone today. The fittings
referred to in yr recent letter
trs. were received, but unfortunately
one of the crates appears. to hv bn
dropped during transit, as many
of the contents are either broken or
cracked [A list of the damaged articles   / NP.
is enclosed and we shall be glad if
you will arrange to send replacements
asap

            Yrs ffy

            D. Brain
            Purchasing Man.

(Key on page 189)

Envelope addressing

Addresses should be typed in the lower half of the envelope with a clear margin above of not less than 38 mm ($1\frac{1}{2}$ inches) for the postage stamps and postmarks. It also helps the Post Office if capital letters are used for the post town. Except in the case of large towns, the county should be included and should be typed in lower case on a separate line. The postcode should appear as the last line of the address with one space between its two parts. It is not punctuated.

The envelopes should be placed on the left-hand side of the machine, so that each may be readily lifted with the left hand to be placed in position and fed in with the right hand by means of the cylinder knob. The name and address should always be typed parallel to the longer side of the envelope.

The quickest and most generally used method of addressing is to use the block style (each line beginning at the same point) and open punctuation. The indented method, whereby each line after the first begins $\frac{1}{2}$ inch to the right of the preceding line, has now largely died out.

Addresses are usually typed in single spacing, but double spacing may be used for large envelopes or if the address is very short.

Courtesy titles, such as *Mrs, Mr, Dr, Ms, The Rev*, etc, should always be included with the name. *Messrs* should be used when addressing a partnership, except when the name of the firm is preceded by the word *The* or a title is included (examples: *Messrs Brown & Jones, Messrs Avis & Co*, but *The Regent Manufacturing Co, Sir James Smith & Co*). A limited company, however, is an incorporated body – a legal person, distinct from any of its members – so that *Messrs* is strictly out of place when used before the name of a limited company, although if personal names are included, *Messrs* is sometimes used in practice.

Initials representing first names should always be followed by a space, but degrees and complimentary initials after a name, such as *MA, BSc, MBE*, are not divided by a space.

Supplementary notes placed on the envelope, such as *Personal, Urgent*, etc, should be typed two line spaces above the name. Internal instructions, such as *First Class*, may be typed in the top left-hand corner.

When *Junior* and *Senior* are required (father and son with the same first name and at the same address) the abbreviations (*Jun* or *Sen*) are placed immediately after the name, as *Mr Arthur Carey Jun* or *Arthur Carey Jun Esq.*

Examples of addresses are given below, and in Exercise 46 a list of names and addresses (all fictitious) are provided for practice. A folded sheet of paper, or any scrap of paper with an area similar to an ordinary envelope, will be suitable for practice. The reverse side of the front of any used envelope also provides good working paper.

Examples of block form of address

```
Sir James Brown & Sons Ltd
345 Rochester Road
CHATHAM
Kent
CH9 2SB
```

```
FOR THE ATTENTION OF MR. J. SMITH

Messrs. James Melhish & Co. Ltd.,
546 Caledonian Road,
BIRMINGHAM.
B9 5TX
```

(Note that in this address the punctuation is 'closed')

URGENT

The Secretary
Modern Engineering Ltd
24-28 Trelawny Road
MANCHESTER
M23 8HG

PERSONAL

J S Penn Esq MA BSc
21 Monteith Road
SOUTHEND-ON-SEA
Essex
S39 38L

Exercise 46

Type the following addresses in block form with open punctuation.

Dr John Laughton, 36 Dudley Road, Derby
    DE6 2LX
Messrs S W Kemp & Sons, 26-30 Booth
    Street, Northampton NN5 5LT
Mr Robert Macdonald, 145 Ladywood Road,
    Portsmouth P01 5RJ
Major Herbert Wilson DSO, Bridge Avenue,
    Reading, Berks RG4 0A2
Professor Sir Albert Lawrence, Melville
    Lodge, Coventry CV1 3AN
    (*Show that the letter is confidential*)
J N C Allerton Esq, 29 Whitmore Road,
    Plymouth PL3 5LU
E Griffiths & Co Ltd, Exeter Street,
    Newmarket NE7 1NJ
Ms W Odell, 63 Charlton Hill, Chester
    CH1 4JN
Mrs A Freeman, J Freeman & Sons Ltd,
    Compton Road, Bournemouth BH8 9NG
    (*Show that the letter is personal*)
Mr Robert Grant Jun, Belmont Road,
    Falmouth FA9 2XC
F T Pemberton & Co Ltd, 42-48 Ashley Road,
    Dover, Kent D09 6SP
The Rev William Gardner MA, The Rectory,
    Grange Road, Norwich N08 5RM

Type the following addresses in block form with closed punctuation.

The Bridge Manufacturing Co. Ltd.,
    Claremont Road, Gloucester.   GL1 5PH
Mrs. Elsie Davidson, 29 Stapleton Road,
    Greenwich, London.   SE13 5NB

13

Memorandums, Forms, Agendas, Minutes

In this chapter various typewritten examples are reproduced, and they provide additional copying practice. Where the examples contain blank spaces for the later insertion of details, it is suggested that one or two copies be made so that the typist can practise filling in different details on the same original.

Memorandums

The memorandum is used for internal communications only, i.e. between members of the same organisation. A memorandum (or memo) form is usually A5 (landscape), although A4 may be used for longer memos. The heading 'Memorandum' is printed or typed at the top of the page. There is no salutation or closure, but spaces are provided for the sender's and recipient's designations or names, the date, and possibly the reference and subject. Care should be taken to ensure that the typed details are lined up with the printed headings. The subject heading may be typed at the left-handed margin or centred or inserted in the space provided. A left-hand margin of 25 mm (1 inch) should be allowed, unless the memo is aligned with the printed matter at the top, which may be less than 25 mm from the edge of the paper.

Specimen layout for a memorandum

MEMORANDUM

To Sales Representative
From Buying Manager   3 October 19--

CHRISTMAS NOVELTIES
The new catalogue of Christmas Novelties is now
available. Please let me know as soon as possible
how many copies you will require for distribution
to your customers.

EMW/JW

Postcards

These are used for business or personal correspondence when the message to be conveyed is short. The recipient's address is typed on the front and the message on the reverse side. Most business firms have their name and address printed on their postcards, but a typed address should be confined to one line if possible and may be separated from the text by a continuous line. As in the case of memos, there is no salutation or closure. Postcards are normally A6 (148 mm × 105 mm) and margins of 1.5 cm ($\frac{1}{2}$ in) to 2.5 cm (1 in) should be allowed depending on the length of the message.

Specimen layout for a postcard

```
"ALLCLEAN" 9 HIGH STREET HITCHIN HERTS   SG5 9PY

EWW/12                          3 November 19--

We are pleased to inform you that your curtains
are now awaiting collection.


                         Manager
```

```
                    POST  CARD



        Mrs J Curtis
        19 Bell Close
        HITCHIN
        Herts
        SG4 9PG
```

Typing forms

Application forms, enrolment forms, questionnaires, etc., should have an adequate number of lines for the information requested. The lines should be double-spaced to provide enough room for the details to be filled in later, and should be typed either with the underscore or the full stop. Not all lines will necessarily be the same length: while an address may require two or three lines, other items such as telephone number or nationality may need only a small space. One space should be left before the lines begin after a word and before another word appearing on the same line.

Specimen layout for a form

```
            FURTHER EDUCATION TEACHER'S CERTIFICATE

            RSA TEFL     *a)   Preparatory Certificate
                          b)   Final Certificate

                          * Delete as necessary

APPLICATION

Miss)
Mrs ) ............... Forenames ...................
Mr  )

Date of birth .................

Address ..........................................

..................................................

........................... Tel no ...........

Date ............... Signature ..................
```

Filling in forms

When filling in forms it is necessary to type over lines which may be dotted or continuous and the paper should be adjusted by using the variable line spacer. No character should cut through a line and care should be taken to see that the 'tailed' letters – **g, j, p, q** and **y** – just clear it. At the same time the typed characters should not 'fly' more than half a line space above the line. It may be necessary to re-align each line of typing if the lines have not previously been produced on a typewriter.

Deletions may be made by a lower or upper case **X** or hyphen.

A completed form

FURTHER EDUCATION TEACHER'S CERTIFICATE

RSA TEFL *a) Preparatory Certificate
          b) XXMXXXXXXXXXXXXXX

          * Delete as necessary

APPLICATION

MXxx)
Mrs) ..SIMPSON........ Forenames Susan June......
MX)

Date of birth .22 June 1943......

Address ...16 Longmead Lane....................

..........Northfields....................

..........MANCHESTER MA6 5BL... Tel no 695318...

Date .3 September 19--. Signature S.J. Simpson.

Circular letters

A company will send out circular letters when it wishes the same letter to go to a large number of people. These letters may be printed, produced on a word processor or otherwise duplicated. Sometimes these letters are formal with no personal details, and may begin 'Dear Member', 'Dear Policyholder', 'Dear Customer', etc. In others, spaces may be left for the later insertion of the name and address, the name in the salutation and the date. Often, however, the date will consist of the month and year only or 'Date as postmark'. Circular letters may be signed in the usual way or left unsigned, but the typed name of the sender and designation should appear underneath, or in more formal letters may be reproduced in print.

A circular letter with spaces for personal details

```
                                    November 19--




Dear

I have pleasure in sending you, with our compliments,
a copy of the TEACHER'S KEY to COMPREHENSIVE ECONOMICS
by Shirley Jones and Peter Walters, published in Oct-
ober at £3.95.

The key provides comprehensive answers to the com-
plete range of questions, exercises and assignments
contained in the main text.

I hope you are pleased with this book.  If you would
like to make any comments or suggestions about it,
I would be happy to hear from you.

Yours sincerely




Linda Power
Publicity Assistant


Enc
```

Form letters

Form letters are similar to circular letters, but contain blank spaces within the body as well for variable items.

Specimen form letter

```
                                    Our Ref .......

                                    Date ..........

Dear Customer

Contract No: /     /        dated
_____

We have pleasure in confirming our acceptance of the
contract signed by you for:

............ Fonansa Machine to be installed at

...................................................

A photostat copy of the Contract is enclosed for
your retention.  This Contract contains all the terms
and conditions which have been agreed.  Please read
it carefully.  If you think anything has been om-
itted you should inform us immediately.

The sum for which the installation is to be insured
pursuant to Clause 5 of the Contract is

£ ..........

Yours faithfully
FONANSA MACHINES LIMITED




Contracts Manager


Enc
```

Letters and forms with tear-off slips

The line to indicate a tear-off slip may be typed with spaced or unspaced dots or hyphens, or by using the underscore. Whichever method is chosen, the line must extend from edge to edge of the paper. There should be at least one clear line space above and below the line, and preferably more if space allows.

Specimen letter with tear-off slip

SEABROOK COMMERCIAL SOCIETY

September 19--

Dear Member

The next meeting of the Society will be held on Saturday 9 October 19-- at the Hastings Hotel, Warren Road, Seabrook. Following lunch, the Manager of one of the local banks will give a talk on the effect of modern technology on the growth of banking services.

Lunch will be served at 12.30 and will cost approximately £4.00, including potatoes, salad bar and sweet, depending on choice. It would be helpful if you would let me know if you wish to have lunch by Wednesday 6 October so that the Hotel can reserve table space for us.

Yours sincerely

Barry Smith
Hon Secretary

To: Mr Barry Smith, 13 Redhill Crescent, Seabrook

I hope to be present at the lunch at the Hastings Hotel on Saturday 9 October at 12.30 pm.

Name .... Tel no ....

Address .... Guests ....

....

Notice of a meeting

This should be sent out well in advance to all those entitled to attend. It states the day, time, place and purpose of the meeting.

Agenda

An agenda is a list of topics to be discussed at a meeting. The topics should be arranged in logical order with the routine business first. An example of a combined notice and agenda appears below.

```
THE AXON CAR CLUB

The Third Annual General Meeting of the Axon Car
Club will be held at the Royal Hotel, Broxbourne,
on Sunday 5 October 19-- at 1500 hours.

A G E N D A

1   Minutes of last meeting.

2   Treasurer's report.

3   Membership fees.

4   Election of new committee members.

5   Date of next meeting.

6   Any other business.




J Stevens
Secretary




Highbourne House
Park Street
Broxbourne, Herts.

12 September 19--
```

Chairman's agenda

In a chairman's agenda the items listed for discussion are typed down the left-hand side of the page, leaving the right-hand side blank for the chairman's notes. A left-hand margin of 1 inch should be allowed. A minimum of treble-line spacing should be allowed for each item. An example appears below.

Specimen layout of a Chairman's Agenda

```
THE AXON CAR CLUB

AGENDA FOR THE THIRD ANNUAL GENERAL MEETING

To be held at the Royal Hotel, Broxbourne, on
Sunday 5 October 19--


1    Minutes of the
     last meeting.



2    Treasurer's Report.



3    Membership Fees.



4    Election of new
     committee members.



5    Date of next meeting.



6    Any other business.
```

Minutes

Minutes of a meeting are the official record of the proceedings of that meeting and are generally typed on A4 paper. The heading always contains the name of the club, firm or society, and the date, time and place of the meeting, and is followed by a list of those present. The items are dealt with in the order that they have been presented on the agenda. Each item is numbered and has either a shoulder heading or a marginal heading. In the example the minutes have been typed with shoulder headings

Specimen layout for Minutes of a meeting

```
THE AXON CAR CLUB

MINUTES OF THIRD ANNUAL GENERAL MEETING

Held at the Royal Hotel, Broxbourne, on
Sunday 5 October 19-- at 1500 hours.

Present:   Mr John Price, Chairman
           Mr James Price, Vice-Chairman
           Mr P Brown
           Mr James Stevens
           Mrs P Smith
           Miss L Jackson
           Mr K R Frost
           Mr B Bacon
           Mr Alan Green, Treasurer
           Mr S P Brown, Secretary

1  NOTICE OF MEETING

   The Secretary read the notice dated 12 September
   19-- convening the meeting.

2  MINUTES OF PREVIOUS MEETING

   The Minutes of the second Annual General Meeting
   held on 3 October 19-- were read, approved and
   signed.

3  TREASURER'S REPORT

   Mr Alan Green reported that the balance of Cash in
   Hand and at the Bank was in a healthy state and
   bearing in mind the proposed outlay for a new dup-
   licator and additional stationery supplied, the
   financial position of the Club could be regarded
   as very satisfactory.
```

4   MEMBERSHIP FEES

It was unanimously decided that the membership fee should be increased by £1.50 to £10.50.

5   ELECTION OF NEW MEMBERS

Mr Alan Brown and Miss Jill Noble were duly elected members of the club.

6   DATE OF NEXT MEETING

The date of the next meeting was fixed for Sunday 3 December 19--.

7   ANY OTHER BUSINESS

The question of time, place and date of next year's Rally was raised and it was decided to postpone any decision until the next monthly meeting.

Chairman

December 19--

14

Display Work

Display work involves the neat and orderly arrangement of the text so that the complete typewritten work will be pleasing to the eye and also easily read. The best examples of display work are to be found in printed matter – chiefly handbills, title-pages, notices, programmes, menus, etc. The printer has a wider selection of typefaces to choose from than most typewriters, but with the skilful use of lower and upper case letters, the underscore, and the variation of spacing between letters, words and lines the typist can secure emphasis in many different ways and display typewritten work attractively.

Use of space

Display work requires skill in the use of space and paper selection. It is not always necessary to centre everything, and indeed modern practice is to 'block' as much as possible in order to save time. However, there are occasions when centring will be necessary and two methods are described.

Refer back to page 14 for the number of spaces across a page of A4 and A5, and take as an example the title of this book:

TEACH YOURSELF TYPING

Insert A5 landscape paper (longer side at top) into the machine, making sure that the left-hand edge is at zero. Set the carriage position indicator at 50 for Elite (half 100), or 41 for Pica (half 82), and then backspace once for every two letters or spaces in the heading. To reach the point at which to start typing the heading, it will be necessary to backspace ten times. Odd letters should always be ignored. Where the material to be typed consists of several centred lines, move the margin stops out of the way and set the tabulator stop at the middle of the page to save time.

Another method of centring is first to count the number of letters and spaces in the heading and then subtract the total from the number of spaces in the width of the paper. For A5 landscape, using Elite type and the same title, 20 is substracted from 100, giving a remainder of 80. This number divided by two shows the point of the scale (40) at which the line should begin.

When the heading is to be placed over matter that has unequal margins, the matter will be arranged immediately over the width of the line of writing, not the width of the paper. If, for example, for binding purposes there is a left-hand margin of 15 and a right-hand margin of 5 (or a writing line of 80 spaces) the above book title would begin at 45 on the scale.

```
ORGANISATIONS SUPPORTING THE ENTERPRISE


        British Aerospace (Aircraft)

        British Aerospace (Dynamics)

            Cadbury Schweppes

        Dickinson Robinson Group

           Harveys of Bristol

             Imperial Group

     Mardon Packaging International

           Newman Industries

             Rolls Royce
```

Vertical centring

Refer again to page 14 and it will be seen that the number of lines *down* a page of A5 landscape is 35. To display the list on page 121 vertically, count the number of lines in the list *including the line spaces*. In this case there are 20. Subtract this figure from 35 and the answer is 15. Divide 15 by two (ignore the half) and the answer is 7. From the top edge of the paper, turn down 7 + 1 (8) line spaces, since the first space will be used up by a line of type.

If a piece of display contains 42 lines, for example, and A4 paper is being used, then the following calculation is necessary: $70 - 42 \div 2 + 1 = 15$. The typing will start on the *fifteenth* line from the top.

Borders and rules

Freak arrangements and the elaborate use of decorative effects are usually avoided in business, but borders and rules can be arranged attractively. The best effect is obtained with little or no ornamentation and extreme simplicity. The following are examples:

```
: : : : : : : : : : : : : : : : : : : : : : : : : : : : : : : : : : : : : : : :

- - - - - - - - - - - - - - - - - - - - - - - - - - - - - - - - - - - - - -

XXXXXXXXXXXXXXXXXXXXXXXXXXXXXXXXXXXXXXXXXXXX
```

Tail pieces
A decorative effect is sometimes desired at the end of chapters or sections, and arrangements of characters suitable for this purpose are:

```
---ooOoo---    ---:::::---    --xxXxx--
```

Display examples

The examples on pages 123–6 are representative of work that can be accomplished on the typewriter.

////////////////////////////////////

THERE   IS   A   FIRE

EVERY   OTHER   MINUTE

You can't be too careful!

////////////////////////////////////

X-X-X-X-X-X-X-X-X-X-X-X-X-X-X-X-X

COUGHS   and   SNEEZES

SPREAD   DISEASES

Stay in your own home and keep warm

X-X-X-X-X-X-X-X-X-X-X-X-X-X-X-X-X

ooo-ooo-ooo-ooo-ooo-ooo-ooo-ooo-ooo

```
            (  give the exact fare
PLEASE  (
            (  name your destination
```

HELP   THE   CONDUCTOR

ooo-ooo-ooo-ooo-ooo-ooo-ooo-ooo-ooo

XX

—— M U S I C ——

1.	Overture	Life's Laughter	Rust
2.	Selection	Mikado	Sullivan
3.	Waltz	Bal Masque	Fletcher
4.	Suite	Carmen	Bizet
5.	Selection	Rose Marie	Friml
6.	Intermezzo	Longing	Haydn Wood
7.	Waltz	Count of Luxembourg	Lehar
8.	Selection	Merrie England	German
9.	Suite	The Royal Fireworks	Handel
10.	Entr'acte	Lovely Night	Ganne
11.	Waltz	The Song is Ended	Berlin
12.	Selection	Scotch Airs	Myddleton

THE ELITE ORCHESTRA
under the direction of
MISS EILEEN NIGHTINGALE

XXXXXXXXXXXXXXXXXXXXXXXXXXXXXXXXXXXXXXXXXXXXXXXXXXXX

KNIGHTS OF THE

ROUND TABLE

FIVE PLAYS FROM THE
ARTHURIAN LEGEND

by

L. du GARDE PEACH

——oOo——

LONDON

Pitman Books Limited

In the menu that appears below, accents are indicated. These should be inserted in black ink if an accent key is not available on the keyboard.

```
:::::::::::::::::::::::::::::::::::::::::::::::::::::::::::::

                        M E N U

                        _____

                         Soup

                  Consommé Royale
                    Thick Oxtail

                         Fish

                 Fillets Lemon Sole
                    Tartare Sauce

                        Joints

        Braised Sweetbreads and Macédoine
            Roast Chicken and Sausage

                      Vegetables

           Spinach         New Potatoes

                        Sweets

            Trifle         Peach Melba

                        Coffee


:::::::::::::::::::::::::::::::::::::::::::::::::::::::::::
```

In Exercise 47 (page 127) various items are given for centring practice; count the number of letters and spaces required for each item and centre each line across a sheet of A4 paper. Allow double spacing between each item, and also centre the exercise vertically. Where there is a space between the letters in a word, leave *three* spaces between the words.

Exercise 47

GREATER LONDON COUNCIL
CITY OF LONDON
BRITISH RAIL
HER MAJESTY'S STATIONERY OFFICE
LONDON TRANSPORT EXECUTIVE
BOARD OF TRADE JOURNAL
POST OFFICE GUIDE
RAILWAY EXECUTIVE
BALANCE SHEET
PROFIT AND LOSS ACCOUNT
LONDON CHAMBER OF COMMERCE
ROYAL SOCIETY OF ARTS
THE TIMES
DAILY EXPRESS
DAILY MAIL
THE PITMAN DICTIONARY OF ENGLISH
  AND SHORTHAND
TEACH YOURSELF BOOKS

15

Tabular work and Accounts

The work in this section is really an extension of the previous instructions regarding the display and the centring of typewritten matter, and deals with the orderly arrangement of columns across a page. Careful planning is required for good results.

The devices used for tabular work vary on different machines, but generally pressing a key or bar moves the carriage to the position at which stops have been set.

Estimating width and depth

Examine the matter to be typed carefully in order to gauge the maximum width and depth required for the complete work. Count the number of characters or characters and spaces in the widest line of each column or heading. An equal number of spaces should be left between each column (three, four or five are best) and these should be included. Subtract the combined total from the number of spaces in the width of the paper (page 14) and divide by two. This is the point at which the left-hand margin stop should be set. Tap the space bar once for each character in the widest line of the first column and for the spaces following, and set a tab stop for the second column. Repeat the procedure until tab stops have been set for all the columns. Both margins will then be equal. On occasion, of course, this tabular work may be placed on a page with ordinary text either starting at the left-hand margin or centred and will not form a distinct item.

Tabular examples

An estimate of the space required for the following example will show how to plan a tab.

FEBRUARY (32)	(46)	(52)	(59)	(66)
Sunday	1	8	15	22
Monday	2	9	16	23
Tuesday	3	10	17	24
Wednesday (5)	4 (5)	11 (5)	18 (5)	25
Thursday	5	12	19	26
Friday	6	13	20	27
Saturday	7	14	21	28

If five spaces are allowed between the columns, the total number of spaces required for the table is 36. For A5 landscape with Elite type, subtract 28 from 100 and divide by two. The answer, 32, is the point for the left-hand margin. Tap the number of letters in the longest word, Wednesday, plus 5 for the following space and set the first tab stop. Tap one for the second column plus 5 and set the tab stop for the second column. Continue until all the stops have been set.

To centre the table vertically, count the number of lines in the table (16), subtract from 35, divide by two (ignore the fraction) and add one. The typing should start on the *tenth* line down from the top.

Type this example in double spacing on A5 paper and then try Exercises 48 and 49 in the same manner.

Note that although main headings may be centred if desired, it is easier and quicker to block them at the left hand margin as shown.

Exercise 48

PRESIDENTS OF THE UNITED STATES 1923-1981

1	Calvin Coolidge	Rep.	1923-9
2	Herbert C Hoover	Rep.	1929-33
3	Franklin D Roosevelt	Dem.	1933-45
4	Harry S Truman	Dem.	1945-53
5	Dwight D Eisenhower	Rep.	1953-61
6	John F Kennedy	Dem.	1961-3
7	Lyndon B Johnson	Dem.	1963-69
8	Richard M Nixon	Rep.	1969-74
9	Gerald R Ford	Rep.	1974-76
10	James Carter	Dem.	1976-81

Exercise 49

List of Subjects

Accountancy	Dietetics	Mathematics	Printing
Advertising	Economics	Metallurgy	Refrigeration
Aeronautics	Elocution	Mineralogy	Salesmanship
Architecture	Engineering	Mining	Shipping
Arithmetic	English	Music	Shorthand
Banking	First-Aid	Needlework	Sociology
Book-keeping	Geography	Optics	Telecommunications
Building	History	Pharmacy	Television
Calculations	Insurance	Photography	Theatre
Chemistry	Investment	Physics	Transport
Commerce	Journalism	Poetry	Typewriting

(Key on page 190)

Table with column headings

Column headings are best typed at the tab stop positions and are regarded as part of the column when making calculations. Leave a clear line space after the heading.

Type the example in double spacing on A5 landscape paper, making the necessary calculations, and then try Exercises 50 and 51 on the same size paper. Exercise 50 may be typed in double spacing, but Exercise 51 should be typed in single spacing. It is suggested that the Arabic and Roman numerals be lined up *to the left*, so that each numeral begins at the same point, blocked under the heading.

Example of a table with column headings

LOCAL GOVERNMENT - DIVISION OF FUNCTIONS

Service	Metropolitan areas	Non-Metropolitan areas	Greater London
Education	District	County	Borough
Personal social services	District	County	Borough
Police and fire services	County	County	GLC
Planning	Shared	Shared	Shared
Highways	Shared	Shared	Shared
Environmental Health	District	District	Borough
Housing	District	District	Borough

Exercise 50

The Grand National

Year	Horse	Jockey	Owner
1972	Well to Do	G Thorner	Capt. T Forster
1973	Red Rum	B Fletcher	Mr N le Mare
1974	Red Rum	B Fletcher	Mr N le Mare
1975	L'Escargot	T Carberry	Mr R Guest
1976	Rag Trade	J Burke	Mr P Raymond
1977	Red Rum	T Stack	Mr N le Mare
1978	Lucius	B R Davies	Mrs D Whitaker
1979	Rubstic	M Barnes	Mr J Douglas
1980	Ben Nevis	C Fenwick	Mr R Stewart Jun
1981	Aldaniti	R Champion	Mrs V Embericos

(Key on page 191)

Exercise 51

<u>Arabic and Roman Numerals</u>

<u>Arabic</u>	<u>Roman small</u>	<u>Roman capitals</u>	<u>Arabic</u>	<u>Roman small</u>	<u>Roman capitals</u>
1	i	I	15	xv	XV
2	ii	II	16	xvi	XVI
3	iii	III	17	xvii	XVII
4	iv	IV	18	xviii	XVIII
5	v	V	19	xix	XIX
6	vi	VI	20	xx	XX
7	vii	VII	30	xxx	XXX
8	viii	VIII	40	xl	XL
9	ix	IX	50	l	L
10	x	X	60	lx	LX
11	xi	XI	70	lxx	LXX
12	xii	XII	80	lxxx	LXXX
13	xiii	XIII	90	xc	XC
14	xiv	XIV	100	c	C

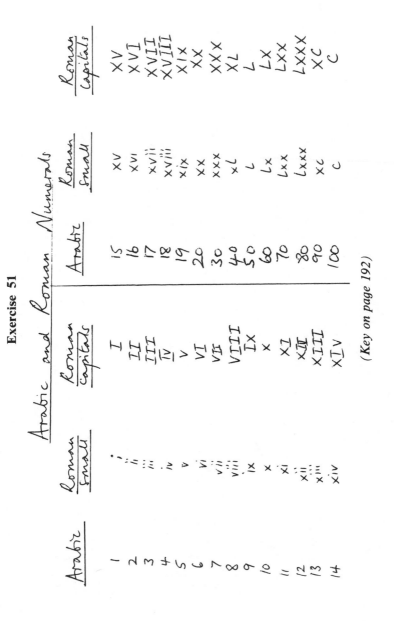

(Key on page 192)

Ruling in ink

Tabular work may be ruled either with the underscore or in ink. In the latter instance, a black ballpoint pen is best. Guide dots (light impressions of the full stop) may be inserted to ensure accuracy. These should be centred between each section to be ruled. The dots for the outside vertical lines should be placed at a point equal to half the number of spaces between the columns. The ruling, which will obscure the guide dots, will be inserted after the paper has been removed from the typewriter. Alternatively, guide dots may be indicated and ruled lines drawn lightly in pencil after the paper has been removed from the machine. Enclose the table first by measuring 5 mm from the typing on all four sides, then with the help of carefully-measured guide dots draw in the remaining vertical and horizontal lines. All traces of pencil markings should be erased after the lines have been inked over. Allow a clear line space above and below horizontal rulings within the table. Column headings in ruled tables should not be underscored and should be in single line spacing.

When there are varying widths of line in a column it is advisable to insert leader dots to link up related items in other columns. These leader dots are best typed in a continuous line, as shown on page 73.

Copy the examples which follow and then type Exercise 52 in single spacing on A5 paper, using the blocked style.

Example of a ruled tab in the blocked style

N E W   B O N D   I S S U E S

INCOME FOR EACH £1000 INVESTED

Age at Commencement	Income received annually	Equivalent Gross Yield to Basic Taxpayer
	£	%
25	73.31	9.37
35	73.43	9.38
45	73.50	9.50
55	74.30	9.60

The same tab fully centred

N E W   B O N D   I S S U E S

INCOME FOR EACH £1000 INVESTED

Age at Commencement	Income received annually	Equivalent Gross Yield to Basic Taxpayer
	£	%
25	73.31	9.37
35	73.43	9.38
45	73.50	9.50
55	74.30	9.60

Exercise 52

THE PRINCIPAL NATIONAL DAILIES

Paper	Proprietors	Circulation in 19.. (millions)
Daily Express	Trafalgar House	2.4
Sun	News International	3.8
Daily Mail	Associated Newspapers	1.9
Daily Mirror	Reed Publishing Holdings	3.6
Daily Star	Trafalgar House	0.9
Daily Telegraph	Daily Telegraph	1.3
Financial Times	Pearson Longman	0.2
Guardian	Guardian and Manchester	0.4
	Evening News	
Morning Star	Morning Star Co-op Society	0.03
The Times	News International	0.3

(Key on page 193)

Typing figures in column form for calculation

Care should be taken to see that units are under units, tens under tens, etc, and that the decimal points are lined up underneath one another. When the blocked style is being used, the currency sign above columns of money should be placed over the first digit. Otherwise it may be placed over the decimal point or over the units column of pounds.

The £ in the total should be typed close up to the figures, and the lines above and below the total should not extend beyond the figures. Use the variable line spacer for the lower total line.

The following examples illustrate the recommended spacing above and below totals:

1	**2**	**3**
Single	*1 ½·line*	*Double*
spacing	*spacing*	*spacing*
£	£	£
396.24	396.24	396.24
364.00	364.00	364.00
25.53	25.53	25.53
15.38	15.38	15.38
£801.15	£801.15	£801.15

Example 1 annotations: Turn up ½ / Turn up 1½ / Turn up ½

Example 2 annotations: (arrows to the total lines)

Example 3 annotations: Turn up 1 / Turn up 2 / Turn up 1

Practise these examples and then type Exercise 53 in single spacing on A5 paper, using the blocked style of layout.

Exercise 53

Electra Machine
Quarterly Sales

Branch	March	June	Sept	Dec
Southampton	136	210	195	187
Portsmouth	125	167	154	170
Liverpool	103	141	139	126
Birmingham	214	230	179	223
Manchester	212	176	194	182
Leeds	317	265	276	284
Sheffield	284	314	237	330
Burnley	147	201	169	229
Middlesbrough	231	192	217	186
Cardiff	246	312	256	306
Swansea	193	224	184	219
Newport	231	189	209	196
Totals	2,439	2,627	2,409	2,638

(Key on page 194)

Accounts

These are usually typed on A4 paper – either on single sheets or on two separate sheets which are joined together when the work is complete. The columns in the account should be separated, if possible, by three character spaces. Calculation for spacing and margins should be made as for tabulation.

The longer side should be typed first so as to determine the line on which the totals should appear. The shorter side will be typed to correspond. A suggested layout for a receipts and payments account, which is the type of account most used by clubs and charitable societies, appears overleaf.

Specimen layout of a Receipts and Payments Account

AXON CAR CLUB

Receipts and Payments Account

for the year ended 30 April 19--

	£	£		£	£
Balance at Bank	2053.10		Bulletin:		
Subscriptions	125.00		Stationery	243.80	
Car Badges	38.70		Postage	192.60	
Bank Interest	5.70		Duplicating	125.00	561.40
			Telephone		36.75
			AGM 19--		64.00
			Xmas Party		110.00
			Car Badges		225.00
			Bank Charges		22.00
			Balance at Bank		1203.35
		£2222.50			£2222.50

16

Technical, Legal and Literary work

Mathematical and scientific expressions

Although special keyboards can be obtained for technical work, it is often necessary for the typist to use a standard keyboard. This work may involve typing mathematical expressions or chemical formulae containing superior or inferior characters (i.e. characters above or below the normal writing line), and writing in some symbols by hand.

Allow a space above and below the expressions when they form part of continuous prose and a space either side of mathematical signs within the expression. Unless a special typewriter is available, the interliner or half-line spacing must be used for the superior and inferior characters. Where there are several of these in a line it is quicker to leave spaces for them, filling them in after the other characters have been typed. Within an expression, characters on one line should be centred between those on two.

Practise the following:

$2x + 3y = 12$

$(x - 7)(x - 2) = x^2 - 9x + 14$

% gain in price $= \dfrac{(6 - 5)}{5} \times 100\% = 20\%$

$2NaHCO_3 - CaCl_2 + 2H_2O + 2NH_3$

$y = \sqrt{2x - 1}$ Area $= \pi R^2 - \pi r^2$

Specifications

A specification contains particulars of work to be carried out. A4 paper is generally used, and the subheadings may be typed in the margin for quick reference. Double- or single-line spacing is permissible, according to the length. The example on page 148 shows one method of layout. As with most documents, there are variations of style and employers' preferences should always be followed.

Wills

A will is a document providing for the distribution or administration of property after the death of the testator. Special parchment is used and the document is typed in double-line spacing. The opening words and the first word of each clause are typed in capitals, as shown in the specimen opposite. The left-hand margin may be set at 24 for Elite type (20 for Pica type) and the attestation clause at 18 for Elite type (15 for Pica type), so as to ensure that there is ample space for the signature of the testator and the witnesses. A4 paper may be used for practice.

Codicils

A simple alteration to a will as it stands can be done by making a codicil. This is nothing more than a supplement to a will. The codicil is typed in similar style to the will as shown in the specimen on page 146.

Endorsements

The endorsement is typed on the back of the document and should contain the date, the names of the parties, a brief description of the contents and sometimes the name of the solicitors by whom the document has been prepared.

Special parchment is used for this document, which can be folded into four, or lengthwise into two. When folding into four, place the paper face upwards and fold it into two by placing the bottom edge level with the top edge and creasing flat; then place the folded edge with the open edges and crease again. The endorsement should be on

Specimen layout of a will

THIS IS THE LAST WILL AND TESTAMENT of me

ALBERT BETHELL of 56 Garner Road Saint Albans

in the County of Hertford Civil Servant

1   I DIRECT the payment of all my just debts

funeral and testamentary expenses by my Executors

hereinafter named

2   I APPOINT my Wife ALICE BETHELL to be

executor and trustee of this my Will

3   I GIVE all my personal chattels unto my

wife the said Alice Bethell

4   I GIVE AND BEQUEATH unto my Brother

THOMAS BETHELL the sum of ONE THOUSAND POUNDS

if he shall be living at my death

5   I GIVE DEVISE AND BEQUEATH all my real and

personal estate whatsoever and wheresoever not

hereby or by any Codicil hereto otherwise

specifically disposed of and of which I can

dispose by Will in any manner I think proper

unto my wife the said Alice Bethell for her own

use and benefit absolutely

6   I REVOKE all former Wills and testamentary

dispositions heretofor made by me

I N   W I T N E S S   whereof I have hereunto

set my hand to this my Will this

day of

One thousand nine hundred and

SIGNED by ALBERT BETHELL the Testator)
in the presence of us both present at)
the same time who in his presence and)
in the presence of each other have   )
hereunto subscribed our names as   )
witnesses   )

Specimen layout of a codicil

THIS IS THE FIRST CODICIL TO THE WILL dated

the   day of

One thousand nine hundred and   of me

ALBERT BETHELL of 56 Garner Road Saint Albans

in the County of Hertford Civil Servant

1   I REVOKE the bequest of ONE THOUSAND POUNDS

to my Brother THOMAS BETHELL

2   I GIVE AND BEQUEATH unto my Cousin JACK FROST

of The Four Winds Breeze Lane Saint Albans

aforesaid the sum of ONE THOUSAND POUNDS

3   IN ALL OTHER RESPECTS I confirm my said Will

I N   W I T N E S S   whereof I have hereunto set

my hand to this my first Codicil this

day of

One thousand nine hundred and

SIGNED by ALBERT BETHELL the Testator)
in the presence of us both present at)
the same time who in his presence and)
in the presence of each other have   )
hereunto subscribed our names as   )
witnesses   )

Specimen layout for an endorsement

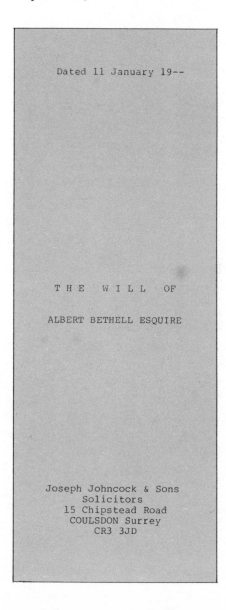

Dated 11 January 19--

THE   WILL   OF

ALBERT BETHELL ESQUIRE

Joseph Johncock & Sons
Solicitors
15 Chipstead Road
COULSDON Surrey
CR3 3JD

Specimen layout of a specification

SPECIFICATION of work required to be
done in the erection of a dwelling house at Epping
for Mr Frank Jones, in accordance with Drawings
prepared by Mr John Dean of 10 High Road, Epping,
the Architect referred to in this specification.

10 May 19--

PRELIMINARY and GENERAL

NOTICES AND FEES   Give all requisite notices to the Local and other
Authorities, obtain all licences, and pay all fees.

SETTING-OUT   The Contractor is to set out the whole of the works in
accordance with the plans; and he will be responsible
for the correctness of the setting-out, and is to amend
the same if it shall be found by the Architect to be
incorrect.

DIMENSIONS ON DRAWINGS

Figured dimensions are, in all cases, to be taken in preference to scale, and the large scale details to be followed in preference to small scale general drawings. In the event of any apparent discrepancy between the drawings or between the drawings and this specification, the Contractor is to ask for an explanation from the Architect before proceeding.

SCAFFOLDING

The Contractor is to supply all scaffolding and plant required for the works.

WATER AND LIGHTING

Pay all charges for water and lighting required during the erection of the building.

Specimen layout of a section of a play

                    S I R   L A U N C E L O T

                    O F   T H E   L A K E

                         ————oOo————

                         CHARACTERS

                    Sir Caradoc   Servant
                    Sir Launcelot   Merlin
                    Queen Morgan le Fay

          A room in SIR CARADOC'S castle with a very heavy-looking
door. There is no window.

          At a table with fruit, wine, etc., QUEEN MORGAN LE FAY
is sitting with SIR CARADOC. A SERVANT pours wine for them.

CARADOC   Leave us!

                    (The SERVANT goes out.)

          Now you may speak freely.

MORGAN   I will. You, Sir Caradoc, have no love for Arthur, my
brother.

CARADOC   I have no more love for him than you.

MORGAN   I hate him! But for him - and Merlin, with his magic
            arts - my husband, King Lot, would have been overlord of
            Britain. Instead of which he has to do homage to him - to
            Arthur!

CARADOC   True.

MORGAN   It is time that Arthur, with his Round Table of knights,
            was exterminated as one stamps out a nest of scorpions.

CARADOC   I should be happy to see it.

MORGAN   You shall be happy.

CARADOC   Arthur is strong, the strongest king in Britain. All
            others are lesser and tributary to him.

MORGAN   Arthur is stronger than any single king, but not stronger
            than all. Together, they could overwhelm him and his knights.

the uppermost side when folded. For a lengthwise fold, place the paper face upwards and fold the left edge over the right edge until the two edges meet, and then crease. The endorsement should be to the right of the crease on the last sheet.

An example of an endorsement for a will is given on page 147.

Dramatic work

This will contain title-page, synopsis of acts and scenery, cast and characters, followed by the spoken parts. A4 paper is used.

Names of speakers are placed alongside their respective parts. All descriptive words not spoken are underlined and typed in single-line spacing. Double-line spacing is used for the dialogue. The example on pages 150–1 is from a short play by L. du Garde Peach, and the title-page of the book from which it is taken was used for the display on page 125. The extract has been typed in traditional style.

Poetry

Single poems should be typed on A4 or A5 paper according to their length, and centrally placed on the page. Single spacing should be used for the verses with two or three clear line spaces between each verse. The title is usually typed in capitals and centred over the writing line.

If successive lines rhyme or there is no rhyme at all, all the lines begin at the margin:

```
                    THE LITTLE DOG'S DAY

      All in the town were still asleep,
      When the sun came up with a shout and a leap.
      In the lonely streets unseen by man,
      A little dog danced.  And the day began.
```

If, however, alternate or certain lines rhyme, or a line is very short, then these may be indented.

SUSPIRIA

```
O would I were where I would be!
   There would I be where I am not:
For where I am I would not be,
   And where I would be I can not.
```

Anon

17

Speed Tests

It may not be within the capacity of every typist to attain a championship rate, but regular practice on the exercises in the earlier sections should have secured a fair speed of operation. High speed will not be attained unless the touch system has been mastered; the eyes must be kept on the copy throughout the test.

Repetition practice

One of the most helpful methods for increasing speed is repetition on straightforward printed matter, which should be typed and retyped several times. The matter selected should be varied, and suitable pieces can be obtained from any book, magazine or newspaper; small print, however, should be avoided. The repetition practice should be abandoned immediately there is any question of partial memorisation and a new piece should then be selected.

'Strokes' and words

When the question of typewriting skill is being discussed it is usually in terms of ability to type at so many words a minute, but it is not generally understood that the word, in this context, is a measured unit. It would not be reasonable for two lengthy words to have the same time value as two short words. Take, for example, 'terminological inexactitude' for 'an untruth'. In the first rendering there are twenty-seven strokes or depressions of keys, including the space bar, and in the second there are only ten strokes or depressions.

Thus, the usual method of counting is to give an average of five strokes for each word. Each depression, whether it be a character key or the space bar, counts as one stroke. If a test containing 2000 strokes is typed in ten minutes, the number of strokes is first divided by five to ascertain the number of words and the result is then divided by the number of minutes to give the word rate for each minute. In this example the rate of typewriting would be forty words a minute.

Deduction for errors

There are various ways of assessing speed tests in relation to the error rate. One method is to allow a maximum of one error per fifty words or part of fifty words typed; another is to deduct ten words from the total typed for each error; and another is to apply an error tolerance. If, for example, a six-error tolerance is allowed in a five-minute speed test, then the speed is calculated on the amount typed up to but excluding a seventh error. These errors may include irregular line spacing, lines too long or too short, paragraphs improperly indented, faulty spacing in relation to punctuation marks, imperfect impressions, transposed letters, words omitted or inserted, 'piling' of letters at the end of a line, irregular left margin, erasures, overtyping, etc.

Exercises

In the tests on pages 156–64 the cumulative stroke count, including a stroke in lieu of space, is given at the end of each line and the total number of words at the end of the test. Should the typing end at an earlier 'stroke' position, it will be an easy matter to find the actual speed at which the section has been typed – first divide the marginal number by five and then by the time taken to reach that point. The result of that division will give the number of words typed each minute.

Remember that, when attempting the tests, speed without accuracy is valueless. It is far better to have good quality than indifferent quantity, and an excellent motto to keep continually in mind is to 'make haste slowly'.

Exercise 54

	Strokes
Long, long ago it was written that "Of making many books	57
there is no end." In those days books were so few that they were	123
quite beyond price. In these modern days, when to come to the	186
end of the book is merely to find that one is at the beginning of	252
another, the reader might add: "And of the reading of many	312
books there is no end." Once one has become a true reader one	375
cannot look upon books with anything but the deepest interest,	438
and, good though the book one is reading may be, there is always	503
the belief that the one waiting to be read will be of the most excep-	573
tional worth. This ever-present desire to pass on to the next book	641
results very often in our not getting out of a book all that it has	709
to offer of worth-while thought or information. The knowledge of	775
this fact causes us to remark, as we put down the book: "I must	840
read that again one of these days", but even as we say the words	906
we know that we shall not in all probability read it again, for	970
the next book is always calling us.	1006

This quick passing from book to book is no matter for surprise in view of the great numbers of books which are published. Books of every kind are at hand—books which simply tell a story; books which set out to teach us about some special subject; books which give an account of some outstanding event of war; books which open out for us the details of the life of this or that person. There are books about the past history of man, the history of nations, the history of industry; books which inform us of the conditions of life in other parts of the world; books relating to the political field; books about science and its relation to industry and to the life of the citizen; books by leaders of modern thought; books in our own language and books in other languages—books and books and books. Naturally, the opinions of the readers of these books differ as much as the books themselves differ. There are those who believe that modern writing has nothing worth-while to offer. Such people go back into the past for their reading material, and tell the world that whenever a new book is published they read an old one.

1069
1135
1203
1270
1333
1404
1469
1535
1605
1673
1741
1805
1871
1939
2001
2067
2130
2141

(428 words)

Exercise 55

	Strokes
The Works Engineer is responsible, through the Works Manager,	62
to the General Manager for the maintenance of all the machinery	126
and plant in the works, and for the personnel concerned there-	189
with. He is also concerned with the introduction of new equip-	253
ment to supplement or replace existing plant, and with the plan-	318
ning of the layout of the shops and the choice of design of the	382
actual machines. In some large works, however, there is a Plan-	447
ning Engineer who is responsible for the last-mentioned duties.	511
The Works Engineer must be able to adapt the plant to meet	570
the demands made by those in charge of actual production, or	631
by those individuals who have planned the works. It sometimes	694
happens, however, that the duties of planner and Works	749
Engineer are combined, and in such a case the official holding this	817
position would do well to invite suggestions from the different	881
repair sections regarding improved methods, both in keeping the	945
plant in the highest state of efficiency, and in the best and quickest	1016
ways of effecting repairs.	1043

It is found advantageous in a large works to employ one or more machine tool inspectors under the Works Engineer on these duties, one inspector undertaking also the duties of Safety Officer.

The machine repair foreman must work in close co-operation with these engineers, reporting to them on the repairs necessary to machines, and indicating whether a machine is worn out, or whether it is fundamentally unsatisfactory. The inspectors are thus frequently able to provide reasons why a certain machine should be replaced, and indications are then made on the plant card in such cases.

In most works today some kind of progress system is in operation, and the Works Engineer should ensure that any breakdown of a machine should be immediately notified to the Progress or Planning Office, as it may be possible to make temporary arrangements to meet the emergency; whereas if the Progress Office were not promptly advised, dislocation of the programme would speedily ensue.

(404 words)

1107
1173
1234
1293
1358
1420
1489
1553
1617
1629
1691
1753
1816
1881
1947
2013
2019

Exercise 56

	Strokes
Goods may be transported by land, sea or air. In this country	63
the greatest transportation of commodities in large bulk is by rail-	130
way, although a very considerable quantity of goods is now trans-	194
ported by fleets of large motor lorries for which trunk systems cover	264
the whole country. There is also a considerable coastwise traffic,	332
again mostly in large bulk. In this case the goods are carried in	399
small vessels known as "coasters" which voyage from one port to	463
another within the United Kingdom. A certain amount of freight	527
is still carried by barge on the inland canal system, but such traffic is	601
gradually decreasing.	624
The transport of goods in overseas transactions is mainly carried	690
out in ships, known as "freighters" which sail to all parts of the	757
world. For goods of high intrinsic value, or where speed is of great	827
importance, much use is now made of the air freight services, but	893
freight charges by air are still relatively high.	944
The packaging, dispatch and transport of goods, particularly	1005
where they are exported to destinations overseas, has now become a	1072

complicated procedure. Considerable knowledge and experience 1134
are required to ensure that the best routes are used and that the many 1205
formalities are complied with. Many of the larger organizations 1270
maintain their own shipping departments where the staff are specially 1340
trained in this kind of work. Traders who would find the mainten- 1405
ance of a special department unjustified will probably avail them- 1470
selves of the service of specialists who are known as forwarding 1535
agents. 1544

Since goods in transit are liable to loss or damage which might 1608
involve both the exporter and importer in heavy financial losses, 1674
these risks are covered by means of insurance which is also a special- 1743
ized business. 1759

Many firms now have their own delivery arrangements and main- 1819
tain fleets of motor lorries which cover a wide radius. This system 1888
has the advantage of being much quicker than transport by the goods 1956
or passenger services of the railways. Goods can be taken direct 2022
from the factory or warehouse of the supplier to the premises of the 2091
purchaser. 2101

(420 words)

Exercise 57

	Strokes
The Stock Exchange, London, is not the only institution of its	63
kind in this country. It is by far the largest of the Stock Exchanges,	135
and the volume of each day's trading stamps it at once as quite	199
the most important. London's age and membership give it the	260
premier position, and its unique system of Jobbers, whereby a	322
more free market exists than in other Exchanges, makes it the	384
centre to which the bulk of investment and speculative business	448
naturally flows. It follows that it is often more convenient for a	516
client who lives, say, in Liverpool to call and consult his Broker	583
there, when discussion on financial matters can freely take place,	650
than to be compelled to enter into voluminous correspondence	711
with a Broker whom he does not know. It is far more satisfactory	777
for the London Broker also, as that personal knowledge and touch	842
so necessary in business must of necessity be lacking under such	907
circumstances.	922

These conditions have resulted in the opening up from time to time of Stock Exchanges in many of the large cities; several towns of importance also have their own representative institutions. Smaller localities can also be recognized as properly constituted for officially conducting Stock Exchange business. The large institutions, situated as near as Birmingham and as remote as Belfast, are known as the Provincial Exchanges.

The Provincial Exchanges, many of them in the heart of the large industrial areas, transact among their own Members an important business, and contribute to London a steady stream of orders. These orders represent business that it is found impossible to execute in the Provincial Exchanges. As far as is practicable, clients' orders are carried out in the local Exchange to which a Stockbroker belongs, the Member there dealing with a fellow-Member. When he is unable so to deal the order is passed through to London, or to another Stock Exchange in the Provinces.

984
1055
1124
1197
1258
1325
1354
1413
1473
1537
1606
1673
1738
1799
1865
1922

(384 words)

Exercise 58

	Strokes
Each age is an age of change, and most people are willing to change	68
with the times, giving up the old and taking what is new. There	133
are, however, a few who cannot or who will not change. At some	197
moment in their lives the willingness to consider new ideas and new	265
methods is lost, and from that time they look back, always back,	330
expressing a longing for the "good old days" and for the happi-	394
ness which for them is part of the past and which does not exist in	462
the present. It is, perhaps, in the country that the desire to keep	531
to the old order of things exists most strongly. Townspeople are	597
used to change: nothing is the same for very long. In the country	665
there is a more lasting quality about things. The little river that	734
runs across the field has run that way for years beyond number, and	802
is likely to continue to do so. The farm labourer would be very sur-	872
prised if the river were not there one day. But a town street is	958
always changing, and people will hardly turn their heads to look	1003
when workmen are pulling down some historic building.	1057

(211 words)

18

Difficult Spellings

Correct spelling, like punctuation, is essential to the production of good typewritten work, and you should never fail to consult a dictionary when there is uncertainty about the correct spelling of any word, and then seek to master it.

A selected list of difficult spellings is given below, and includes common words which often cause problems – such as *accommodate*, *gauge* and *seize* – as well as words which are in general business use. It is recommended that each page of the list should be typed, in order to impress the correct spelling on the mind. The meaning of the words is equally important, and a dictionary should be consulted where there is any doubt.

abhor	acknowledge	aggrieved
abhorred	acquiesce	aghast
abolish	acquire	agreeable
abscess	adhere	allege
accede	adherence	allegiance
accept	adjournment	alliance
access	admissible	allotment
accessible	adolescent	aluminium
accommodate	advantageous	amateur
accommodation	advertise	ambiguity
accumulate	advertisement	ameliorate
achieve	aerial	amicable
achieving	affect	ampersand
aching	aggregate	analogous

analyse
analysis
anomalous
appal
appalling
apparent
apparently
appendix
appropriate
argument
ascend
asset
assuage
asterisk
atrocious
auspicious
authentic
authenticity
auxiliary

bankruptcy
banquet
basically
bazaar
belief
believable
believe
beneficiaries
beneficiary
benefit
benefited
bias
bilateral
biography
bona fide
book-keeping
boycott
brilliance
brittle
budget
budgeting
buoy

bureaucracy
bureaucrat
by-election
by-law
by-product

cafeteria
calamitous
camouflage
canister
career
casualty
catalogue
catarrh
catastrophe
ceiling
changeable
chaos
chaotic
chargeable
chauffeur
chronological
coefficient
coincide
coinciding
collateral
colleague
colloquial
collusion
combustible
commitment
committal
compatibility
compatible
comprehensible
comprehensive
compulsory
conceivable
conglomerate
connoisseur
conscientious
conspicuous

consummate
contentious
continent
controversy
conversation
conversion
corduroy
corollary
corroborate
corruptible
counterfeit
credible
crucial
cul-de-sac
curriculum

debacle
debar
debarred
debutante
decree
decreeing
defensible
defer
deferred
deficiency
deficient
demarcation
dependant (of)
dependent (on)
deprecate
depreciate
descendant
destructible
deterioration
deter
deterrent
develop
development
dial
dialling
dilemma

discern
discernible
discreet
discretion
discretionary
dissatisfaction
disseminate
disservice
dissuade
doubtful
dubitable
dynamic

earnest
eavesdrop
ecclesiastical
ecstasy
edible
efficient
eligible
elucidate
embarrass
enamel
enamelled
encumbrance
encyclopaedia
entrepreneur
epitome
equanimity
equitable
equivalent
erstwhile
et cetera
etiquette
evaporate
exacerbate
exchange
exchangeable
excusable
excuse
exorbitant
extraneous

eyewitness

facial
facile
fallacious
fatigue
feasible
February
fictitious
floatation
focus
formally
formerly
  (previously)
fortuitous
freeing
fulfil
fulfilled
fulfilment

gauge
gauging
gazetteer
glossary
gratuitous
guarantor
gullible
gymnasium

haphazard
harass
hazardous
heterogeneous
honorable
honorary
humorist
humour
hygiene
hypothesis

idiosyncrasy
illiteracy

illiterate
illusion
imminent
immovable
impracticable
impromptu
incognito
incur
incurred
independence
indict
indictment
infinitesimal
ingenious
install
instalment
interim
irreducible
irresistible
itinerary

janitor
jargon
jeopardise
jewellery
judiciary
judicious
juxtaposition

kilogram
kilometre
kilowatt
kudos

label
labelled
laborious
liaison
libel
libellous
litigation

magnanimous
magnate
magnetise
maintenance
maisonette
malingerer
malleable
malpractice
manage
manageable
manoeuvre
marshalled
massacre
misapprehend
mis-statement
monetary
mortgage
mystery

naïve
necessary
necessitate
nomenclature
nondescript
nonplussed
notable
notice
noticeable
nowadays
nullify

obituary
obsession
occur
occurrence
omission
omit
omitted
onerous
ophthalmic
ostentatious
outrageous
overrate

panel
panelled
paraffin
parallel
paralleled
parcel
parcelled
pastime
pecuniary
penultimate
perceivable
perceive
perceptible
peremptory
permissible
permit
persecute
persuade
persuasive
pessimism
pharmaceutical
phenomenal
plagiarise
pneumatic
postcard
posthumous
practice (noun)
practise (verb)
precede
predecessor
prefer
preferred
principal (chief)
principle
proceed
process
proffer
programme (*but*
    computer
    program)
pronounce
pronounceable
pronunciation

propitious
pseudonym
psychology
purchasable
pursue

quandary
quantitative
quarrel
quarrelled
queue

rateable
readdress
rearrange
receivable
reciprocate
recur
recurrence
removable
rendezvous
reprehensible
rescind
rescission
résumé
reversible
rhythm
rival
rivalled
rudimentary

sceptic
scepticism
scrutineer
secession
segregate
seizable
seize
silhouette
simultaneously
skiing
skilful
sophisticated

sovereignty
spontaneous
stationary (not moving)
stationery (en- velopes, etc)
statistician
stencilled
stereotyped
subsidiary
succeed
succession
succint
sue
suggest
suggestible
suing
supercilious
supersede
surreptitious

susceptible
synonymous
synthesis

tautology
teetotaller
temporary
tinge
tingeing
trademark
transfer
transferable
transferred
tunnel
tunnelled

ubiquitous
unanimous
unilateral
unkempt

unnecessary
unparalleled
utilitarian

vapour
vaporise
vehicular
veil
vigorous
vigour
voracious

wilful
witticism

yardstick

zoology

19

Abbreviations

Abbreviations are shortened forms of words and phrases – consisting in many cases only of initials – which have become established by common usage. The following list is not exhaustive, but includes most of the abbreviations in general business use and shows their meanings.

The use of the full stop will depend on whether open or closed punctuation is employed. Note, however, that certain signs and symbols should never take a full stop, for example the £ or $ sign, the ampersand (&) and @ (at). In addition, full stops should not be used after abbreviations of units of measurement, such as ft, mm and kg.

& and (ampersand)
@ at, for
A1 first class, first rate
a. a. r. against all risks
ab init. *ab initio* (Latin), from the beginning
abt about
a/c, acct account
A/C current account
AD *anno domini* (Latin), in the year of our Lord
ad., advt advertisement
ad lib. *ad libitum* (Latin), at pleasure
ad val. *ad valorem* (Latin), according to value

AGM Annual General Meeting
agt agreement; agent
a.m. *ante meridiem* (Latin), before noon
amt amount
anon. anonymous
ans. answer
A/P accounts payable
appro. approval, approbation
approx. approximate
A/R accounts receivable
A/S account sales
a.s.a.p. as soon as possible
asst assistant
av., ave average

BA   Bachelor of Arts
bal.   balance
b/d   bring (brought) down
B/D   Bank Draft
B/E   bill of exchange
b/f   bring (brought) forward
bk   book
B/L   bill of lading
B/P   bill payable
B/R   bill receivable
Bro., Bros   brother, brothers
B/S   balance sheet; bill of sale
BSc   Bachelor of Science
bx, bxs   box, boxes

c   cent(s)
C   centigrade, celsius
C/A   Capital Account
carr. pd   carriage paid
carr. fwd   carriage forward
cat.   catalogue
cc   cubic centimetre; carbon copy
c/d   carried down
cf.   compare
c/f   carried forward
C & F   cost and freight
ch., chap.   chapter
chq.   cheque
c.i.f.   cost, insurance and freight
cm   centimetre
C/N   credit note
Co.   Company
c/o   care of; carried over
COD   cash on delivery
col.   column
comm.   commission
cont.   continued
co-op   co-operative
cr.   credit, creditor
CS   Civil Service

cum div.   with the dividend
c.w.o.   cash with order

D/A   Deposit Account
DB   Day Book
D/D   Demand Draft
Deb.   Debenture
dely, d/y   delivery
dept   department
dft   draft
disc.   discount
div.   dividends; division
D/N   Debit Note
do.   ditto (the same)
doz.   dozen
D/P   documents against payment
dr.   debtor, debit
Dr   Doctor
d/s   days after sight
D.V.   *Deo volente* (Latin), God Willing

ea.   each
ed.   edition, editor
e.g.   for example (*exempli gratia*)
enc.   enclosure(s)
entd   entered
E&OE   errors and omissions excepted
EPT   Excess Profit Tax
esp.   especially
Esq.   Esquire
est.   established; estimated
et al.   *et alia* (Latin), and others
ETA   estimated time of arrival
etc.   *et cetera* (Latin), and the rest
ETD   estimated time of departure

et seq.   *et sequentia* (Latin), and the following
ex.   without
exch.   exchange
ex div., x. div.   without dividends
ex int.   not including interest
exors   executors
exp.   express
exs   expenses

f, fr.   franc(s)
F, Fahr.   Fahrenheit
f.a.a.   free of all average (used in marine insurance)
FAO   for the attention of
f.a.q.   free alongside quay; fair average quality
f.a.s.   free alongside ship
fcp, fcap   foolscap
f.d.   free docks
f.i.f.o.   first in, first out
fig[s]   figure(s)
f.i.t.   free of income tax
fo, fol.   folio
FO   Firm Order
f.o.b.   free on board
f.o.r.   free on rail
fp.   fully paid
fr.   from
frt   freight
ft   foot, feet
fwd   forward

g   gram(me)
GA   general average (insurance)
gen.   general
GM   General Manager
GMT   Greenwich Mean Time
Gov.   Governor
Govt.   Government
gr.   grain, grammar

gr. wt.   gross weight

HMSO   Her Majesty's Stationery Office
HO   Head Office
Hon.   Honorary, Honourable
h.p.   horse power
HP   hire purchase
HQ   headquarters
hr, hrs   hour(s)

ib, ibid.   *ib idem* (Latin), in the same place
IB   Invoice Book
IBI   Invoice Book Inwards
i/c   in charge
i.e.   *id est* (Latin), that is
I/F   insufficient funds (banking)
IMF   International Monetary Fund
Inc.   incorporated
ins.   insurance
inst.   instant, current month
int.   interest
inv.   invoice
IOU   I owe you
ital.   italics
IQ   Intelligence Quotient
J/A   Joint Account
JP   Justice of the Peace
Jun., Jr   Junior

kg, kilo   kilogram(me)
kl   kilolitre(s)
km   kilometre(s)
kw   kilowatts

£   pound sterling
l, lit.   litre(s)
lat.   latitude
lb   pound (weight)
l.c.   lower case

L/C Letter of Credit
Led. Ledger
LGA Local Government Authority; Local Government Area
l.i.f.o. last in, first out
long. longitude
Ltd limited

m metre(s), minutes, million
max. maximum
MC Master of Ceremonies
m/d months after date
med. medium
mem., memo. memorandum
Messrs *Messieurs* (French), Gentlemen
mfg manufacturing
mfr manufacturer
mg milligram
mgr manager
min. minimum, minute
MIP Marine Insurance Policy
ml millilitre(s)
mm millimetre(s)
Mme Madame
MO Medical Officer; money order
MP Member of Parliament; Military Police
m.p.h. miles per hour
m/s months after sight; metre per second
ms(s). manuscript(s)
MSc Master of Science

n.a. not available
N/A no advice; not acceptable (banking); not applicable
NB *nota bene* (Latin), mark well, note well

nem. con. *nemine contradic-ente* (Latin), no one contradicting
N/F no funds (banking)
nil *nihil* (Latin), nothing
N/m no mark
N/O no orders (trading)
nom. nominal
NP Notary Public
NPV no par value
nr near

% per cent
%0 per thousand
o/a on account of
o/c over charge; officer commanding; out of charge
o/d on demand
O/D overdraft, overdrawn
OK all correct
O&M Organisation and Methods
o/p out of print
op. cit. *opere citato* (Latin), in the work cited
opp. opposed, opposite
OR owner's risk
ord. ordinary
o/s out of stock; outstanding

p., pp. page, pages
p.a. *per annum* (Latin), yearly
PAYE pay as you earn (taxation)
p.c. per cent; post card
PC Police constable
p/c price current
p.c.b. petty cash book
pcl parcel
pcs pieces
pd paid
per by

per capita by the head
per pro, pp *per procurationem* (Latin), on behalf of
pkg. package
P & L Profit and Loss
Plc Public Limited Company
p.m. *post meridiem* (Latin), afternoon or evening
p/n promissory note
P.O. postal order; post office
pp. parcel post
p. & p. postage and packing
pr, pr. pair, price
pref. preference, preferred
prima facie at first sight
Prof. Professor
pro forma as a matter of form
pro tem. *pro tempore* (Latin), for the time being
PS postscript
PTO please turn over
PV per value

qu. query, question
quan. quantity
qr quarter

R/D refer to drawer (banking)
re. with reference to, concerning
rec(t) receipt
recd received
ref. reference
reg., regd registered
rep. report; representative
retd returned
rly railway
rm ream
R/p reply paid
RSVP *Repondez, s'il vous plait* (French), please reply

$ dollar (money)
SB sales book
sch. school; schedule
sec. second
sgn sign(ed)
S/N shipping note
soc. society
spec. specification, speculation
sq. square
SS steamship
St. Saint; street; station
std standard
STD Subscriber Trunk Dialling
stet let it stand
stg sterling (money)
stk stock

TMO telegraph money order
TO, t/o turnover
Tr. Trustee
TT telegraphic transfer

u.c. upper case
ult. *ultimo* (Latin), last month; ultimatum
u/w underwriter

v., vs versus; against
var. variety
VAT Value-added tax
VHF very high frequency
via by way of, through
viz. *videlicet* (Latin), namely
vol. volume

W/B Waybill
w.e.f. with effect from
whf wharf
wk(s) week; weeks
w.p.m. words per minute
wt, wgt weight

x.d. ex dividend (without dividend)

x.int. ex interest (without interest)

yr(s) year(s)

yrs yours

Keys to the Exercises

Key to Exercise 32

The question of the original home of the tea plant is by no means settled, the point at issue being whether the true home of the plant is in China or Assam. Because the tea plant attains extraordinary luxuriance in Assam, it could be argued that this is its natural home. However, it has been noticed that plants introduced into new countries have flourished as well as native plants.

A Japanese legend ascribes to China the honour of being the home of the tea plant and there are certain references to the plant in the writings of a Chinese author who lived about 2,700 BC. A Chinese commentator on this ancient author, writing in the fourth century BC, calls attention to the mention of the plant and adds that a beverage could be obtained from the leaves by adding hot water. It appears that the plant was used entirely as a medicine until AD 550 when it became a popular beverage.

Key to Exercise 33

Originally the work of professional accountants was confined
chiefly to the checking of arithmetical accuracy of the detailed records of transactions in books of account, the
agreement of the Trial Balance, and the preparation of
accounts - in fact, to what may be described as 'accountancy'
work; but nowadays the all-important part of a professional
accountant's work is that of auditing.

The difference between accountancy and auditing is not
clearly understood by many business men, it being thought
that if accounts are prepared by a professional accountant
he necessarily guarantees their accuracy. This, however, is
far from being the case. If an accountant is instructed
merely to prepare accounts from a set of books, he would be
acting simply as an expert accountant, and not in any way as
an auditor.

Key to Exercise 34

The effect that colour has on us and our feelings is being
looked at more and more closely.   In America it was found
that output in a factory went up 8 per cent when rest areas
were painted a horrible bright green because staff couldn't
bear to stay too long.   Workmen considered some big dark
boxes too heavy to haul until they were painted a lighter
colour.

Yellow is believed to be happy and free; orange outgoing
and warm; blue calming and cool, giving a feeling of security and peace.   Red is exciting to some people but can be
oppressive as well.   It has the most direct impact on the
senses and can make people argue so beware of painting a
room in your home red.   Violet with its make-up of blue and
red can cause one to hesitate.   Which colour takes the
helm - the aggressive red or the calmer blue?

Key to Exercise 35

To write is not necessarily to communicate with another
mind. Writing is primarily expression - and whoever has
made use of it to record what he has felt and thought and
done, or as a means of meditation, will know already that
such exercises are in themselves amply rewarding. He will
know also that the practice of writing to oneself is invaluable.

What are the main advantages of written expression? As
against thinking in the head, which is more likely to be
fragmentary, the written word gives a fixed form to the
underlying thought it expresses. The writer can then judge
whether the thought itself is of value and whether its
expression is adequate.

Key to Exercise 36

Mass production is the name given to a method of manufacture
in which one standard pattern takes the place of a variety
of shapes and sizes. The principle is not new, and its advantages have been known in industry for a very long time.
During the last few decades, however, a number of manufacturers have carried the method to its logical conclusion,
which is: one kind of article only produced in a single factory. The advantages claimed for the mass production method
are many. Chief among them is the possibility of adjusting
the operations of manufacture so that there may be the
completest economy in man and machine power in every part of
the work. The best known example of mass production is the
motor car, an article which is complex and made of many parts.
The principle adopted is that of a series of factories side
by side in each of which a different part is made. Those
parts pass on in continuous streams and on completion pass in
to an assembly shop. Here the cars are gradually built up
from the beginning to the end at an almost incredible rate of
speed. From end to end the great saving of thought, time,
and labour arises from the absolute similarity of one car to
all others of the same class. Every worker repeats ad infinitum the operation that falls to him, till not a movement
is wasted or a fraction of time is lost.

Key to Exercise 37

Libel is a term which in popular use includes any statement of a defamatory character made by one person of another. Technically, however, it includes any statements in writing or other more or less permanent record. Legally, spoken words are termed slander, and from the point of view of the person complaining the distinction is important. In the case of slander it is usually necessary to prove that as a result of words spoken the party claiming to be injured has suffered special damage, whilst in libel such proof is not necessary. Even in slander words imputing unfitness, dishonesty or incompetence in business or tending to prejudice a man in his public calling are actionable without proof of special damage. Even a public company may bring an action when defamation amounts to impeachment of its conduct of business.

Words spoken or written may on the face of them be innocent but they may have a hidden meaning understood by others. In such cases the libel is by innuendo.

Fair comment on matters of public interest may be a justification of defamatory statements, and if the comment is fair and reasonable there is no libel. The standard of what is fair is not fixed but if the motive is pure the statement is generally justified, and the matter is a question of fact for the jury. Another justification is that the words spoken or written are true. This is a defence which must be proved to the hilt or the plea itself will aggravate the offence.

Key to Exercise 38

(Reference)

(Today's date)

The General Manager
Bridge Machinery Company
Garner Road
STOCKPORT
Cheshire
SK5 6EP

Dear Sir

As you know, we are having a great deal of trouble with
the Crosford machine which you installed last month. Our
maintenance engineer has followed your suggestions, but
the results are still very unsatisfactory.

In the circumstances, we shall be pleased if you will
arrange to send your expert this week if possible to inspect the machine and advise us.

Yours faithfully

P L Jones
Manager

Key to Exercise 39

(Reference)

(Today's date)

The General Manager
Brick & Steel Limited
Palace Wharf
EDGWARE
ED7 3LT

Dear Sir

FLATS AT MAIN AVENUE, WILLESDEN

You are invited to tender for the erection of a block of
flats at the above location for The Housing Trust Limited,
and I shall be pleased if you will let me know as soon as
possible whether you desire to tender, in order that quantities may be sent to you. The drawings of the proposed
work may be inspected at my office on making an appoint-
ment.

Tenders are to be delivered to me within one month.

Yours faithfully

Key to Exercise 40

(Reference)

(Today's date)

Mr John Andrews
Messrs Andrews & Son
14-16 Church Street
LIVERPOOL
LI 3AA

Dear Mr Andrews

Thank you for your recent enquiry. We are enclosing our
latest catalogue and price list, and are asking our representative to call on you next week to discuss the best
word processor for your needs.

In the meantime, we shall be pleased if you will give us
additional particulars by filling in the attached form and
returning it as soon as possible to this office.

Yours sincerely

A Jones
Sales Manager

Encs

Key to Exercise 41

(Reference)

(Today's date)

The Sales Manager
Climax Steel Co Limited
209-211 Chesterfield Street
HALIFAX
SI 0SA

Dear Sir

We are sending herewith our Order No 608 for Steel Angles
and Channels, which we urgently require in connection with
an important contract. Delivery is of extreme importance
and we should like to have the material in our Works by next
weekend if possible.

The bars to be supplied would be of ordinary commercial
quality, and while the quantity is large you will see that
only three sections are involved. In these circumstances
we have no doubt you will be able to meet our requirements
in regard to delivery.

Please let us know immediately the very best you can do for
us.

Yours faithfully
R & S BUILDERS

A D Jones
Assistant Manager

Enc

Key to Exercise 42

(Reference)

(Today's date)

Mr J W Webb
Chief Design Engineer
Messrs John Smith & Company
901 London Road
MAIDSTONE
MA5 6LR

Dear Mr Webb

Owing to the steady growth of our business we are moving to
larger premises in Main Street, Slough, Bucks at the end of
this month. The site is a particularly good one, in the
heart of this industrial centre, within easy reach of
London and the M4 Motorway. The transport difficulties
which we have experienced in the past will now be reduced
to a minimum, and early deliveries ensured.

The new factory will be fully automated with a resulting
increase in both the quality and quantity of our output.

We trust that you will be patient with us during this transitional period. Any delays should be minimal only and we
expect to achieve full production again within five weeks.

May we take this opportunity of expressing our thanks for
your confidence in the past and we hope that the improvements we shall introduce will lead to even more business.

Yours sincerely

J Simpson
General Manager

Key to Exercise 43

(Reference)

(Today's date)

The General Manager
J Finn & Company Limited
534 Western Road
SWINDON
SN2 5DA

Dear Sir

We should be pleased to assist you to the best of our
ability to replenish your stock on advantageous terms.

The enclosed illustrated catalogue contains concise
details of the many household goods that we think would
interest you.

We have just been appointed agents for the manufacturers
of a British-made oil heater which is both cheap and
satisfactory and your special inquiry reaches us at the
right moment. The heater is obtainable in various models
at prices from £35.50 and has the following special points:

1   It gives a maximum heat of twice as much warmth as other
     heaters in its class.

2   The flame is easily adjustable to any reasonable height,
     giving greatly increased comfort and economy.

3   With the patent burner any excess of oil is drained
     back into the tank, ensuring safety and complete elimin-
     ation of smoke and smell.

4   The heater burns at full capacity for a cost of approx-
     imately 5p an hour.

If you will let us know your requirements we will ask our
representative to call on you.

Yours faithfully

T R Cockburn
Sales Manager

Enc

Key to Exercise 44

(Reference)   (Today's date)

Mr. William Mortimore,
The Cedars,
Manor Crescent,
HARROGATE
HA7 9PQ

Dear Mr. Mortimore,

We are very glad that you have written to us to query some
of the items on the bill that we sent to you, since we
always urge customers to let us know when they do not feel
satisfied on any matter.

With regard to the oil which you state is very much dearer
than before, we would mention that you agreed a better grade
of oil would conserve the engine power for a longer period,
and you authorised us to supply you with a more expensive
brand.

Concerning the labour charge of £10.00 for repair to the
front bumper, this was undertaken at the request of your son.

We regret that we are unable to reduce the charge for the
materials, as this was previously agreed upon as being
reasonable.

                         Yours sincerely,

                         P. J. Jones,
                         Service Manager.

Key to Exercise 45

(Reference)   (Today's date)

Messrs. Benham & Brown,
417 Selwyn Road,
LONDON.
E13 OPY

Dear Sirs,

    We confirm our conversation on the telephone today.
The fittings referred to in your recent letter were received, but unfortunately one of the crates appears to
have been dropped during transit, as many of the contents
are either broken or cracked.

    A list of the damaged articles is enclosed and we
shall be glad if you will arrange to send replacements
as soon as possible.

                 Yours faithfully,

                      D. Brain,
                Purchasing Manager.

Key to Exercise 49

LIST OF SUBJECTS

Accountancy	Dietetics	Mathematics	Printing
Advertising	Economics	Metallurgy	Refrigeration
Aeronautics	Elocution	Mineralogy	Salesmanship
Architecture	Engineering	Mining	Shipping
Arithmetic	English	Music	Shorthand
Banking	First-Aid	Needlework	Sociology
Book-keeping	Geography	Optics	Telecommunications
Building	History	Pharmacy	Television
Calculations	Insurance	Photography	Theatre
Chemistry	Investment	Physics	Transport
Commerce	Journalism	Poetry	Typewriting

Key to Exercise 50

THE GRAND NATIONAL

Year	Horse	Jockey	Owner
1972	Well to Do	G Thorner	Capt T Forster
1973	Red Rum	B Fletcher	Mr N Le Mare
1974	Red Rum	B Fletcher	Mr N Le Mare
1975	L'Escargot	T Carberry	Mr R Guest
1976	Rag Trade	J Burke	Mr P Raymond
1977	Red Rum	T Stack	Mr N Le Mare
1978	Lucius	B R Davis	Mrs D Whitaker
1979	Rubstic	M Barnes	Mr J Douglas
1980	Ben Nevis	C Fenwick	Mr R Stewart Jun
1981	Aldaniti	R Champion	Mrs V Embericos

Key to Exercise 51

ARABIC AND ROMAN NUMERALS

Arabic	Roman small	Roman capitals	Arabic	Roman small	Roman capitals
1	i	I	15	xv	XV
2	ii	II	16	xvi	XVI
3	iii	III	17	xvii	XVII
4	iv	IV	18	xviii	XVIII
5	v	V	19	xix	XIX
6	vi	VI	20	xx	XX
7	vii	VII	30	xxx	XXX
8	viii	VIII	40	xl	XL
9	ix	IX	50	l	L
10	x	X	60	lx	LX
11	xi	XI	70	lxx	LXX
12	xii	XII	80	lxxx	LXXX
13	xiii	XIII	90	xc	XC
14	xiv	XIV	100	c	C

Key to Exercise 52

THE PRINCIPAL NATIONAL DAILIES

Paper	Proprietors	Circulation in 19-- (millions)
Daily Express	Trafalgar House	2.4
Daily Mail	Associated Newspapers	1.9
Daily Mirror	Reed Publishing Holdings	3.6
Daily Star	Trafalgar House	0.9
Daily Telegraph	Daily Telegraph	1.3
Financial Times	Pearson Longman	0.2
Guardian	Guardian and Manchester Evening News	0.4
Morning Star	Morning Star Co-op Society	0.03
Sun	News International	3.8
The Times	News International	0.3

Key to Exercise 53

ELECTRA MACHINE

Quarterly Sales

Branch	March	June	Sept	Dec
Southampton	136	210	195	187
Portsmouth	125	167	154	170
Liverpool	103	141	139	126
Birmingham	214	230	179	223
Manchester	212	176	194	182
Leeds	317	265	276	284
Sheffield	284	314	237	330
Burnley	147	201	169	229
Middlesbrough	231	198	217	186
Cardiff	246	312	256	306
Swansea	193	224	184	219
Newport	231	189	209	196
Totals	2,439	2,627	2,409	2,638

Index